PROGRAMMER'S

MICROSOFT® QUICKPASCAL®

▫ ▫ ▫ ▫ ▫

KRIS JAMSA

PUBLISHED BY
Microsoft Press
A Division of Microsoft Corporation
One Microsoft Way
Redmond, Washington 98052-6399

Copyright © 1990 by Kris A. Jamsa

All rights reserved. No part of the contents of this book
may be reproduced or transmitted in any form or by any means
without the written permission of the publisher.

Library of Congress Cataloging-in-Publication Data
Jamsa, Kris A.
   Microsoft QuickPascal: programmer's quick reference / Kris Jamsa.
     p.   cm.
   ISBN 1-55615-243-4 : $6.95
   1. Pascal (Computer program language)   2. Microsoft QuickPascal
  (Computer program)   I. Title.
QA76.73.P2J35   1990
005.26'2--dc20   89-29758
                                                                     CIP

Printed and bound in the United States of America.

1 2 3 4 5 6 7 8 9   RARA   3 2 1 0

Distributed to the book trade in Canada by General Publishing Company, Ltd.

Distributed to the book trade outside the United States and Canada by Penguin
Books Ltd.

Penguin Books Ltd., Harmondsworth, Middlesex, England
Penguin Books Australia Ltd., Ringwood, Victoria, Australia
Penguin Books N.Z. Ltd., 182–190 Wairau Road, Auckland 10, New Zealand

British Cataloging in Publication Data available

Microsoft® and MS-DOS® are registered trademarks of Microsoft
Corporation.

Project/Technical Editor: Dail Magee, Jr.
Manuscript Editor: Wally Parker

Contents

Introduction   1

PART I: Starting QuickPascal   3

Getting Started with QuickPascal   3
Using QuickPascal's On-Line Help   5
Customizing the QuickPascal Editor   6
Using the Command Line Compiler   10

PART II: Using QuickPascal   13

Keywords   13
Predefined Global Variables   14
Units   15
Operators   16
Data Types   17
Object-Oriented Considerations   23
Compiler Directives   25
Conditional Compilation   29

PART III: QuickPascal Functions and Procedures   33

Index to Functions and Procedures by Unit   257

Introduction

This quick reference guide provides information about Microsoft QuickPascal that you use on a daily basis. It is divided into three parts.

Part I explains how to start QuickPascal and how to take advantage of QuickPascal's pull-down menus and on-line help. You will also learn how to customize the QuickPascal editor and how to compile programs both from within QuickPascal and from the MS-DOS command line using the QPL compiler.

Part II discusses several key QuickPascal concepts such as data types, keywords, compiler directives, units, operators and their precedence, and conditional compilation. It also contains a brief discussion of QuickPascal object-oriented programming.

Part III discusses each QuickPascal function and procedure in detail. In many cases a complete programming example is provided to illustrate the routine's use.

The following notational conventions apply to entries in this guide:

Convention	Meaning
italics	Italicized names are placeholders for information you must supply, such as a numeric value.
[*item*]	Items enclosed in square brackets are optional. (You should not type the brackets. However, the notation for Pascal sets, strings, and arrays does use square brackets; in such cases you must type the brackets.)
[*item1* ! *item2*]	Vertical bars indicate a choice between two or more items.

(continued)

continued

Convention	Meaning
<data type>	Names enclosed in angle brackets specify categories of data types; for example, *<integer type>* means that you can use any integer type such as Byte, Integer, Word, ShortInt, or LongInt.
item...	An ellipsis following an item indicates that you can add more items of the same form. (Do not type the ellipsis.)

PART I:
Starting QuickPascal

GETTING STARTED WITH QUICKPASCAL

After you've installed QuickPascal, you can start the QuickPascal environment by entering the following commands at the system prompt:

```
CD \QP
QP
```

QuickPascal is called a *programming environment* because it provides an editor, a compiler, and a debugger built into one fast and easy-to-use program. When you enter the environment, QuickPascal displays an editing window. You can begin entering a new Pascal program in this window, or you can load an existing program from disk and edit it in another window.

QuickPascal provides several different pull-down menus. If you are using a mouse, you can simply click on a menu and then select the option you want. If you are using the keyboard, you access the menus by pressing the Alt key. When you press the Alt key, the first letter of each menu name lights up. You select a specific menu by pressing the corresponding letter. After you select a menu, you can use the direction keys to select an option from the menu, or you can simply type the highlighted letter that corresponds to the option. To cancel a menu, press the Esc key.

The following briefly describes each QuickPascal menu.

File menu: The QuickPascal File menu lets you open a program file stored on disk, save the current program to disk, print the current program, or exit QuickPascal.

Edit menu: The QuickPascal Edit menu lets you cut and paste program text from one location in a program to another or from one program to a different program.

View menu: The QuickPascal View menu lets you control your screen display. QuickPascal lets you open as many as nine windows for editing. Using the View menu, you can move, size, and close windows. The View menu's Close option is useful for leaving the QuickPascal on-line help facility.

Search menu: The QuickPascal Search menu lets you quickly locate, and optionally replace, a word or phrase in your program. Rather than make several similar program changes by hand, you can save considerable editing time by using the Search menu options.

Make menu: The QuickPascal Make menu lets you compile your program, whether it consists of one module or multiple modules.

Run menu: The QuickPascal Run menu lets you control the way QuickPascal executes your program. In most cases, you simply press the F5 function key, directing QuickPascal to compile and execute your program. If you are debugging a program, however, you might want to execute the program one statement at a time. The Run menu gives you this capability.

Debug menu: The QuickPascal Debug menu lets you set breakpoints at which execution stops in your program so that you can examine the values of key variables. Using the QuickPascal debugger, you can eliminate the need for debug Writeln statements in your programs.

Options menu: The QuickPascal Options menu lets you customize the QuickPascal environment for your specific needs. Several of the options on the Options menu parallel the compiler directives discussed in this reference guide. If you are unsure about an entry's function, refer to the compiler directives.

Help menu: The QuickPascal Help menu provides access to the QuickPascal Advisor, the on-line help system. The following section explains the help system in greater detail.

USING QUICKPASCAL'S ON-LINE HELP

QuickPascal provides two on-line help features, the QuickPascal Express and the QuickPascal Advisor.

The QuickPascal Express

The QuickPascal Express is an on-line tutorial that walks you through the QuickPascal environment, teaching you how to use the editor, how to compile and execute programs, and how to use the debugger. The tutorial takes only a few minutes, and it will save you considerable time and effort as you use QuickPascal to develop your programs. To run the tutorial, enter the following commands at the system prompt:

```
CD \QP
LEARN
```

If you are using a floppy-disk-based system, insert the disk labeled "Microsoft QuickPascal Express" in drive A and enter the following commands at the system prompt:

```
A:
LEARN
```

The QuickPascal Advisor

QuickPascal's second on-line help package is the QuickPascal Advisor. You can access it from within the environment by using the Alt+H key combination to select the QuickPascal Help menu.

The Contents option: The Contents option on the Help menu displays a table of topics covered by the Advisor. Using your keyboard arrow keys, position the cursor on the entry you want and press F1. QuickPascal displays a screenful of information on the topic, which you can scroll through. You can print the current Help window using the Print option on the File menu (Alt+F P). To exit the Advisor, use the View menu's Close option to close the Help window (Alt+V C).

The Index option: The Index option on the Help menu lets you select topics listed in alphabetical order. By default, QuickPascal displays the topics that begin with the letter A. To choose a different letter, simply place the cursor in the alphabet bar on the letter you want and press Enter. When the new list of topics appears, use the arrow keys to place the cursor on the name of the topic of interest and then press F1. As before, when the information is displayed, you can print it and close the Help window or return to the Index or the Contents option to choose additional help.

"Context-Sensitive" Help

The QuickPascal Advisor provides "context-sensitive" help. If you are editing your program and you want to get help on a specific topic—say, the Writeln procedure—you can simply place the cursor anywhere on the word *Writeln* and press F1. The Advisor will display information about Writeln, bypassing the Help menu. By examining the current screen contents before it displays help information, the Advisor takes the current screen context into account.

Example programs: In addition to help on QuickPascal types, keywords, functions, and procedures, the Advisor contains over 50 complete QuickPascal programs. You can access these programs from the Example Programs option on the Contents menu.

CUSTOMIZING THE QUICKPASCAL EDITOR

As noted, the QuickPascal environment includes an editor, a compiler, and a debugger. Most programmers have a favorite editor that they use to write programs. As you will see, QuickPascal can mimic several popular editors and even lets you create your own.

Selecting an Alternative Keyboard Interface

If you examine the files in the QuickPascal subdirectory, you will find several with the extension KEY. These files contain the keyboard combinations for several popular text editors. QP.KEY is the default editor. To select a different editor, simply start QuickPascal using the /k switch, as shown here:

```
QP /k:BRIEF
```

In this case, QuickPascal uses the keyboard interface for the BRIEF text editor.

Defining Your Own Keyboard Interface

Instead of selecting one of the predefined keyboard interfaces, you can define your own keyboard interface with the QPMKKEY program.

The QPMKKEY program lets you convert a binary KEY file to an ASCII file so that you can edit the KEY file's current keyboard definitions, customizing them for your own use. Using QPMKKEY again, you can convert the ASCII file back to a binary file so that you can use it with the QuickPascal /k switch. When you use QPMKKEY, you must include the following options:

Option	Description
-c	Specifies the type of conversion—binary to ASCII (ba) or ASCII to binary (ab)
-i	Specifies the input file
-o	Specifies the output file

To begin the customizing process, convert the file QP.KEY to an ASCII file so that you can read the current keyboard definitions:

```
QPMKKEY -c ba -i QP.KEY -o MYKEYS.TXT
```

This command directs QPMKKEY to convert a binary file (QP.KEY) to an ASCII file (MYKEYS.TXT). When QPMKKEY completes execution, you can print the file MYKEYS.TXT for a list of the current editor key definitions.

Next, use your favorite editor to edit MYKEYS.TXT to customize the keyboard combinations you want for editing. After you are satisfied with the changes, you can use QPMKKEY again to convert this ASCII file to a binary KEY file:

```
QPMKKEY -c ab -i MYKEYS.TXT -o MYKEYS.KEY
```

After QPMKKEY creates the key file, you can start QuickPascal using your own keyboard definitions:

```
QP /k:MYKEYS.KEY
```

Keyboard Combinations in QP.KEY

By default, QuickPascal uses the key file QP.KEY. The following list describes the default editor keyboard combinations. (Note that this list does not include all of QuickPascal's keyboard combinations; for a comprehensive list, consult the QuickPascal Advisor.)

Function	Key Combination
Menu Control	
Activate the menu bar	Alt or F11
Cancel	Esc or F12
Cursor Control	
Move left one character	Left or Ctrl+S
Move right one character	Right or Ctrl+D
Move left one word	Ctrl+Left or Ctrl+A
Move right one word	Ctrl+Right or Ctrl+F
Move to start of line	Ctrl+Q S
Move to end of line	End or Ctrl+Q D
Move to first character in line	Home
Move to first character in next line	Ctrl+J
Scroll left one screenful	Ctrl+PgUp
Scroll right one screenful	Ctrl+PgDn
Move up one line	Up or Ctrl+E
Move down one line	Down or Ctrl+X
Scroll up one line	Ctrl+Up or Ctrl+W
Scroll down one line	Ctrl+Down or Ctrl+Z
Move to top of screen	Ctrl+Q E
Move to bottom of screen	Ctrl+Q X
Scroll up one screenful	PgUp or Ctrl+R
Scroll down one screenful	PgDn or Ctrl+C
Move to start of program	Ctrl+Home or Ctrl+Q R

Function	Key Combination
Move to end of program	Ctrl+End or Ctrl+Q C
Set bookmark 0	Ctrl+K 0
Set bookmark 1	Ctrl+K 1
Set bookmark 2	Ctrl+K 2
Set bookmark 3	Ctrl+K 3
Move to bookmark 0	Ctrl+Q 0
Move to bookmark 1	Ctrl+Q 1
Move to bookmark 2	Ctrl+Q 2
Move to bookmark 3	Ctrl+Q 3
Move to matching brace, parenthesis, or bracket	Ctrl+]

Editing Functions

Function	Key Combination
Delete character at cursor	Ctrl+G
Delete character to left of cursor	Ctrl+H
Delete remainder of word at cursor	Ctrl+T
Delete current line	Ctrl+Y
Erase to end of line	Ctrl+Q Y
Toggle insert mode	Ins or Ctrl+V
Mark beginning of text block	Ctrl+K B
Mark end of text block	Ctrl+K K
Delete text block	Del
Cut text block to Clipboard	Ctrl+K Y
Copy and paste text block	Ctrl+K C
Move text block to location of cursor	Ctrl+K V
Split current line, leaving cursor at end of first line	Ctrl+N
Split current line, leaving cursor at beginning of second line	Ctrl+M
Insert tab character	Ctrl+I
Enter control character	Ctrl+P
Undo previous edit	Ctrl+Q L
Find word or phrase	Ctrl+Q F
Repeat last find	Ctrl+L
Change word or phrase	Ctrl+Q A
Interrupt command in progress	Ctrl+U or Ctrl+Q U or Ctrl+K U

USING THE COMMAND LINE COMPILER

In addition to letting you compile and execute programs from within the QuickPascal environment, QuickPascal provides a command line compiler, QPL.COM, that lets you compile programs from the DOS prompt.

Assume, for example, that you have just edited the program TEST.PAS using your favorite editor or word processor. From the system prompt, you can compile the program by using the following command:

```
QPL TEST.PAS
```

If QPL encounters syntax errors in your program, it will display the corresponding error messages on your screen. If your program compiles successfully, QPL will generate an EXE file.

The QPL program supports several command line switches that work as compiler directives. The following table briefly summarizes each.

Switch	Description
/D *symbol*	Defines a symbol for conditional compilation. To define several different symbols, simply separate the symbols with semicolons.
/E *directory*	Defines the subdirectory in which the executable file is to be placed.
/P *directory*	Defines a list of subdirectories in which QPL will search for a source file if it fails to locate the source file in the current directory. To search several different directories, simply separate the directory names with semicolons.
/I *directory*	Defines a list of subdirectories in which QPL will search for an include file if it fails to locate the include file in the current directory. To search several different directories, simply separate the directory names with semicolons.

Switch	Description
/O *directory*	Defines a list of subdirectories in which QPL will search for an assembly-language object file if it fails to locate the object file in the current directory. To search several different directories, simply separate the directory names with semicolons.
/U *directory*	Defines a list of subdirectories in which QPL will search for a QuickPascal unit (QPU) file if it fails to locate the unit file in the current directory. To search several different directories, simply separate the directory names with semicolons.
/R	Directs QPL to rebuild the program (recompile all modules of a multiple-module program).
/B	Directs QPL to build the program (recompile all *modified* modules of a multiple-module program).
/$A[+ǀ−]	/$A+ Directs QPL to word-align variables for better performance on 80x86 processors.
/$B[+ǀ−]	/$B− Directs QPL to generate program code that performs lazy Boolean evaluation. If a condition requires two parts ((A > 1) AND (B > 2)) and the result of the condition is known after the first part (if A is less than or equal to 1, the entire condition is false), there is no need to evaluate the entire condition.
/$D[+ǀ−]	/$D+ Directs QPL to include debugging information for tracing and breakpoints. Debugging information slows program execution and creates a larger EXE file.
/$F[+ǀ−]	/$F+ Directs QPL to force all function and procedure calls to FAR calls.
/$G[+ǀ−]	/$G+ Directs QPL to generate instructions for the 80286. Although the program will then run faster on an 80286 machine, it will not run on an 8088.

(continued)

continued

Switch	Description
/$I[+ : −]	/$I− Directs QPL to disable its I/O checking and error handling after each I/O operation. Most programs should leave I/O checking enabled.
/$L[+ : −]	/$L+ Directs QPL to include local variable information for use in debugging. This information produces a larger EXE file; you should remove the directive in the final version of the program.
/$M[+ : −]	/$M+ Directs QPL to ensure that memory is allocated for an object before the object's method is called. Programs using object-oriented techniques should always use /$M+.
/$N[+ : −]	/$N+ Directs QPL to generate instructions for 80x87 math coprocessors. Although the program will then run faster on a system that has a coprocessor, it will not run on a system without one.
/$R[+ : −]	/$R− Directs QPL to disable range checking on string, array, and enumerated types. After your program is working correctly, you should disable range checking to improve your program's performance.
/$S[+ : −]	/$S− Directs QPL to disable stack checking. After you have successfully tested your program, you should disable stack checking to improve your program's performance.
/$V[+ : −]	/$V+ directs QPL to perform strict type checking, forcing the actual and formal parameters for string parameters passed as type VAR to match identically in length.
/$M *stacksize, minheap, maxheap*	Defines the program's stack, minimum heap, and maximum heap sizes. The default values are 16,384; 0; and 655,360.

PART II:
Using QuickPascal

KEYWORDS

A keyword is a word that QuickPascal reserves for special use, such as BEGIN, which marks the beginning of a block of related statements, or END, which marks the last statement in a block. Because QuickPascal reserves its keywords for its own use, your programs cannot use keywords for function, procedure, and variable names. The following is a list of QuickPascal's keywords.

ABSOLUTE	IF	RECORD
AND	IMPLEMENTATION	REPEAT
ARRAY	IN	SET
BEGIN	INHERITED	SHL
CASE	INLINE	SHR
CONST	INTERFACE	STRING
CSTRING	INTERRUPT	THEN
DIV	LABEL	TO
DO	MOD	TYPE
DOWNTO	NIL	UNIT
ELSE	NOT	UNTIL
END	OBJECT	USES
EXTERNAL	OF	VAR
FILE	OR	WHILE
FOR	OVERRIDE	WITH
FORWARD	PACKED	XOR
FUNCTION	PROCEDURE	
GOTO	PROGRAM	

PREDEFINED GLOBAL VARIABLES

A global variable is a variable that your program's functions and procedures can access throughout the entire program. QuickPascal defines several global variables that contain specific values such as the current text attributes or the state of extended Ctrl+Break checking. The following table describes QuickPascal's global variables.

Variable Name (Unit)	Description
CheckBreak (Crt)	True if extended Ctrl+Break checking is enabled.
CheckEOF (Crt)	True if program tests for end-of-file on input.
CheckSnow (Crt)	True if the Crt output routines wait for CGA video retrace to eliminate snow.
DirectVideo (Crt)	True if the Crt output routines perform direct memory-mapped output.
DosError (Dos)	The error status level of the last Dos unit service.
Input (System)	File pointer to the DOS standard input. If your program does not specify an input file for Read and Readln, Input is used.
LastMode (Crt)	The current text mode. By using LastMode, a program can quickly change from graphics mode to the previous text mode.
Lst (Printer)	File pointer to the system printer.
Output (System)	File pointer to the DOS standard output. If your program does not specify an output file to Write or Writeln, Output is used.
TextAttr (Crt)	The current text foreground color (bits 0–3), background color (bits 4–6), and the blink attribute (bit 7).

Variable Name (Unit)	Description
WindMax (Crt)	Stores the row and column coordinates of the current text window's lower right corner. The low-order byte contains the column; the high-order byte contains the row.
WindMin (Crt)	Stores the row and column coordinates of the current text window's upper left corner. The low-order byte contains the column; the high-order byte contains the row.

UNITS

QuickPascal provides five units that contain functions and procedures your program can use to perform specific tasks. The following table summarizes the QuickPascal units.

Unit	Description
System	The default unit. Contains the functions and procedures common to Pascal compilers. QuickPascal automatically includes the System unit in your program.
Crt	Contains functions and procedures that enhance screen output and keyboard input capabilities.
Dos	Contains functions and procedures that access the DOS system services.
MSGraph	Contains functions and procedures that implement the Microsoft graphics library.
Printer	Contains the Lst variable declaration for printer output.

Part III of this quick reference guide lists each QuickPascal function and procedure with its corresponding unit. To use a routine that resides in a QuickPascal unit, you must specify the unit in the USES clause. For example, the following program uses the ClrScr procedure, which is contained in the Crt unit.

```
PROGRAM AccessUnit;
USES
  Crt;  { contains ClrScr procedure }

BEGIN
  ClrScr;
  Writeln('This text is in the upper left corner');
END.
```

The USES clause must immediately follow the program name and appear before your program's variable, procedure, and function declarations.

OPERATORS

All programming languages support mathematical operators for addition, subtraction, multiplication, and division. The following table summarizes the QuickPascal operators.

Unary Operators	Description
@	Returns a pointer to an identifier
NOT	Bitwise NOT
+	Identity
−	Sign inversion

Multiplication Operators	Description
*	Multiplication
/	Floating-point division
DIV	Integer division
MOD	Remainder of integer division
AND	Bitwise AND
SHL	Left shift
SHR	Right shift

Addition Operators	Description
+	Addition or concatenation
−	Subtraction
OR	Bitwise OR
XOR	Bitwise exclusive OR

Relational Operators	Description
=	Equal
<>	Not equal
<	Less than
<=	Less than or equal to
>	Greater than
>=	Greater than or equal to
IN	Member of set

Logical Operators	Description
NOT	Boolean NOT
AND	Boolean AND
OR	Boolean OR
XOR	Boolean exclusive OR

To ensure that expressions are evaluated consistently, QuickPascal assigns a precedence order to its operators. QuickPascal performs the operation with the highest precedence first. If two operators have the same precedence, QuickPascal performs the operations from left to right. The following table summarizes QuickPascal's operator precedence.

Higher	@ NOT
	* / DIV MOD AND SHR SHL
	+ - OR XOR
Lower	= <> < <= > >= IN

DATA TYPES

Every variable your program defines must be of a specific data type. QuickPascal provides a wide range of data types. Each type supports a particular set of operators and stores a particular range of values. The following briefly describes QuickPascal's data types.

Simple Types

A simple type stores a single value at any given time, as opposed to an array or record that can store several values. The QuickPascal simple types include string, ordinal, and real types.

String types: QuickPascal provides the STRING and CSTRING data types. The STRING type is used more often. When you create a variable of type STRING and assign a character string to it, QuickPascal stores the string's current length in the first byte of the string. The CSTRING data type, on the other hand, stores strings in the same format as the C programming language, indicating the last character in the string by following it with the null character (ASCII 0).

Assuming that your program assigns the string *QuickPascal* to both a STRING and a CSTRING variable, the variables store the characters as shown in Figure 1.

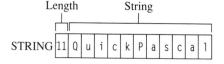

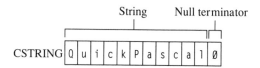

Figure 1. *The byte structure of STRING and CSTRING variables.*

Most programs use the STRING type exclusively. Several graphics programs in the MSGraph unit, however, require CSTRING. By default, variables of both type STRING and CSTRING can store as many as 255 characters. To reduce unused memory, your program can declare a string size less than the maximum, as shown here:

```
VAR
  strVar: STRING[100];    { 100 characters maximum }
  cstrVar: CSTRING[100];
```

Ordinal types: The QuickPascal ordinal types include Boolean, Char, integer, subrange, and enumerated types. An ordinal type is a type with an ordered finite set of values.

A Boolean data type stores a true or false value.

A Char data type stores a single ASCII character.

QuickPascal provides several integer data types. Each type supports a different range of values, as described in the following table.

Type	Minimum Value	Maximum Value
Byte	0	255
Integer	−32,768	32,767
LongInt	−2,147,483,648	2,147,483,647
ShortInt	−128	127
Word	0	65,535

A subrange type contains a contiguous set of values of any ordinal type. A subrange specifies the range of values a type can store. The following TYPE statement creates two subrange types.

```
TYPE
  SignedByte = -128..127;
  Uppercase = 'A'..'Z';
```

After you define a subrange type, your program can declare variables of that type.

An enumerated type is an ordered list of values. For example, the following type statement creates an enumerated type named Languages.

```
TYPE
  Languages = (Pascal, C, BASIC, FORTRAN, COBOL);
```

After you define an enumerated type, your program can declare variables of that type or refer to members within the type, as shown here:

```
IF (codeVariable = FORTRAN) THEN
  { statements }
```

Pascal does not let your program perform I/O with enumerated types.

Real types: QuickPascal also provides several real, or floating-point, data types. Each data type supports a particular precision, or degree of accuracy, as described in the following table.

Type	Range	Significant Digits
Comp	−9.2E+18 to 9.2E+18	15–16*
Double	5.0E−324 to 1.7E+308	15–16
Extended	3.4E−4932 to 1.1E+4932	15–16*
Real	2.9E−39 to 1.7E+38	11–12
Single	1.5E−45 to 3.4E+48	7–8

* Using the {$N+} compiler directive increases the number of significant digits by 4.

Structured Types

A structured type differs from a simple type in that the structured type can store several values at one time. QuickPascal provides the following structured types: ARRAY, RECORDS, FILE, SET, and class (or OBJECT).

QuickPascal arrays let your programs store one or more values of the same type. To create an array, your program must specify the array name, the index values for the array, and the data type, as shown in these examples:

```
VAR
  scores: ARRAY[1..100] OF Byte;
  temps: ARRAY[-150..150] OF Integer;
  workers: ARRAY[1..someConstant] OF WorkerRecord;
```

A record allows your program to store a collection of values of dissimilar types. To create a record type, use the keyword RECORD and specify the fields that the record is to contain.

```
TYPE
  StockItem = RECORD
    name: STRING;
    quantity: Integer;
    cost: Real;
    reorder: Boolean;
  END;
```

You can then declare one or more variables of that type.

```
VAR
  item: StockItem;
```

To assign a value to a particular field of a record, follow
the record name with a period and the name of the desired
field.

```
item.name := 'Monitor cover';
item.quantity := 42;
item.cost := 29.95;
item.reorder := False;
```

QuickPascal supports three types of files: text, untyped
(binary), and typed. Text files contain standard ASCII
characters. To create a file pointer to a text file, use the
predefined type Text as shown here:

```
VAR
  filePointer: Text;
```

An untyped file is a binary file. Common binary files are
EXE and COM program files. To create a file pointer to an
untyped file, your program simply specifies the type FILE.

```
VAR
  filePointer: FILE;
```

A typed file is a file containing values of a specific data
type such as Integer, Real, or even RECORD. To create a
file pointer to a typed file, your program must specify the
file's data type after the keyword FILE.

```
VAR
  filePointer: FILE OF Integer;
  empPointer: FILE OF EmpRecords;
```

A set is an unordered collection of values. Programs often
create sets of enumerated or character types. QuickPascal
provides set operators that perform set union, intersection,
and difference and that also test for set membership. The
following declaration creates a variable capable of storing a
set of characters.

```
VAR
  symbols: SET OF Char;
```

After the set variable exists, your program can assign
values to it as follows:

```
symbols := ['A'..'Z'];
symbols := ['A','B','C'];
symbols := ['A'..'Z'] + ['a'..'z'];
```

A class is an object-oriented data type that contains an object's data fields as well as the procedures and functions (called methods) that can work with the object. The following definition creates a class of type ClassRoom that contains the information an instructor uses to track student test scores and determine grades.

```
TYPE
  ClassRoom = OBJECT
    studentCount: Byte;
    grades: ARRAY[1..maxStudent, 1..maxTest]
      OF Byte;
    numTest: Byte;
    Procedure ClassRoom.Initialize;
    Procedure ClassRoom.GetAverage: Real;
  END;
```

Reference Types

QuickPascal provides two reference types, a procedure type and a pointer type. A procedure type is a pointer to a function or procedure.

A pointer type contains the segment and offset address of a variable or routine in memory. QuickPascal supports both typed and untyped pointers. A typed pointer is a pointer to a specific data type. An untyped pointer is a pointer to a memory location without regard for the type of the value stored there. The following declaration creates an untyped pointer and two typed pointer variables.

```
TYPE
  UntypedPtr: Pointer;
  IntPtr: ^Integer;
  RealPtr: ^Real;
```

The caret (^) before the data type tells QuickPascal that the variable is a pointer. Keep in mind that a pointer stores a memory address. To access the value stored at the memory address, you must dereference the pointer value using the caret, as shown here:

```
RealVariable := RealPtr^;
```

The trailing caret directs QuickPascal to access the value at the memory location the pointer contains. If you omit the caret, QuickPascal will attempt to assign the pointer's value—which is an address—to the variable, which will result in a type error.

OBJECT-ORIENTED CONSIDERATIONS

QuickPascal expands Pascal's standard capabilities by providing the class data type for use in object-oriented programming. (An object is a particular instance of a class.) A class is a data type similar to a record in that each contains one or more fields. But a class type also contains a list of functions and procedures known as methods. Methods determine the operations a program can perform on an object. A class can also inherit data structures and methods from a previously defined class.

To define a class type, use the following syntax.

```
TYPE
  ClassName = OBJECT
    field1: FieldType;
    { additional fields }
    ProcedureName[(formal parameters)];
    FunctionName[(formal parameters)]: ReturnType;
    { other methods }
END;
```

For example, the following definition creates a class named Lamp and defines the fields and methods for it.

```
TYPE
  Lamp = OBJECT
    state: Byte; { 0 off, 1 on, 2 dim }
    watts: Byte;
    location: String;
    PROCEDURE Lamp.TurnOff;
    PROCEDURE Lamp.TurnOn;
    PROCEDURE Lamp.Dim;
END;
```

After you create a class, your program must define the class's methods (procedures and functions). In this case, the program must create the procedures Lamp.TurnOff,

Lamp.TurnOn, and Lamp.Dim. The Lamp.Dim procedure is shown below.

```
PROCEDURE Lamp.Dim;
BEGIN
  { statements }
END;
```

An object is a variable of a specific class type. Your program declares objects following the keyword VAR.

```
VAR
  nightLamp: Lamp;
  deskLight: Lamp;
```

Within your program, you must allocate memory for each object by using the New procedure.

```
New(nightLamp);
New(deskLight);
```

After each object exists, you can manipulate the objects as shown here.

```
deskLight.watts := 45;
deskLight.TurnOn;          { calls method }
nightLamp.watts := 60;
nightLamp.Dim;             { calls method }
```

When your program is finished with an object, the program can release the memory allocated for the object with the Dispose procedure.

```
Dispose(nightLamp);
```

QuickPascal also lets your program create subclasses. A subclass is a class type that changes or adds new fields or methods. Using the Lamp example, several lamps can be on timers. Rather than create a completely new class, your program can define a subclass of the Lamp class that inherits the same fields and members. In this case, the subclass is named TimerLamp.

```
TYPE
  TimerLamp = OBJECT(Lamp)
    timeOn: LongInt;
    timeOff: LongInt;
    PROCEDURE TimerLamp.SetTimer;
    PROCEDURE TimerLamp.Dim; OVERRIDE;
END;
```

A subclass automatically inherits all the parent class's fields; consequently, the class definition does not have to explicitly list the fields. In this case, the class definition adds two new fields and a new method. The last line includes the keyword OVERRIDE. Most people want lamps on timers to be either on or off but not dim. Here the TimerLamp class defines its own Dim procedure, which overrides the Dim procedure defined by the parent class. The TimerLamp class uses the procedures TurnOn and TurnOff that it inherits from the parent class.

COMPILER DIRECTIVES

A compiler directive instructs the compiler to perform specific processing. For example, programs can use the {$I+} or {$I–} compiler directive to enable or disable I/O checking. A compiler directive that turns a specific feature on or off is called a switch directive. The QuickPascal compiler supports the switch directives discussed in the following sections.

Switch Directives

The **{$A+}** compiler directive tells QuickPascal to align constants and variables larger than one byte on word boundaries in memory. Word alignment improves a program's performance on the 80x86 processors. It does not affect the 8088 processor's performance. By default, QuickPascal uses word alignment: {$A+}.

The **{$B+}** compiler directive tells the compiler not to generate code for lazy Boolean evaluation. Consider the following condition:

```
IF ((a < 5) AND (b > 0)) THEN
  statement;
```

If the first condition fails, the entire condition fails because of the AND operator. Lazy Boolean evaluation directs the program to quit evaluating an expression as soon as the outcome is known. In this case, if *a* is greater than or equal to 5, there is no reason for the program to evaluate the second expression. By default, QuickPascal enables lazy evaluation: {$B–}.

The **{$D+}** compiler directive tells the QuickPascal compiler to insert debugger information in your program that allows you to single-step through the program statements while debugging. The additional instructions produce overhead that makes the program run more slowly. If your program is executing successfully, you should disable debugger information with {$D–}. By default, QuickPascal places the debugger instructions in your program: {$D+}.

The **{$F+}** compiler directive instructs QuickPascal to generate FAR calls for the procedure and function calls that follow. When this directive is disabled, QuickPascal determines whether to use a FAR or a NEAR call based on the routine's location. Routines in other units are always FAR calls. FAR calls execute more slowly than NEAR calls because they require a change of segment registers. The default setting is NEAR calls: {$F–}.

The **{$I+}** compiler directive enables IO checking. Programs can disable IO checking, perform an IO operation, reenable IO checking, and then test IOResult to control their own IO error processing. By default, QuickPascal enables IO checking: {$I+}.

The **{$L+}** compiler directive causes QuickPascal to include local symbol information in your executable program that lets your programs display watch values while debugging. After your program is working successfully, you should remove the local symbol information using {$L–}. When you recompile, your executable program file size will decrease. By default, QuickPascal includes local symbol information: {$L+}.

The **{$M+}** compiler directive tells QuickPascal to ensure that memory for an object has been allocated before the object's method is called. Programs using QuickPascal's object-oriented capabilities should enable method checking. By default, QuickPascal disables method checking: {$M–}.

The **{$N+}** compiler directive directs QuickPascal to generate code for an 80x87 math coprocessor. When you enable this directive, the resulting executable program will run only on systems that have math coprocessors. If you attempt to execute the program on a system that doesn't have a coprocessor, a run-time error occurs. When you disable coprocessor support, the resulting program will not use the coprocessor—even if one is present. By default, QuickPascal disables coprocessor support: {$N−}.

The **{$R+}** compiler directive tells QuickPascal to perform range checking to ensure that array and string expressions do not exceed a variable's boundaries and that assignments to scalar and subrange types are within the correct range. When range checking is enabled, a range violation results in a run-time error. Range checking produces significant overhead, which makes a program run more slowly. Most programmers enable range checking only when they are testing a program. By default, QuickPascal disables range checking: {$R−}.

The **{$S+}** compiler directive tells QuickPascal to check stack space before every procedure and function call to ensure that sufficient space exists for local variables. If stack space is insufficient, a run-time error occurs. Stack checking produces considerable overhead, which makes your program run more slowly. After your program is working successfully, you should disable stack checking using {$S−}. By default, QuickPascal enables stack checking: {$S+}.

The **{$V+}** compiler directive directs QuickPascal to perform strict type checking on character strings passed as variable parameters. When VAR string checking is enabled, the actual and formal parameters for strings passed by reference must be identical. By default, QuickPascal enables VAR string checking : {$V+}.

If your program uses several compiler switch directives, you can place all the directives in one statement as shown in this example:

```
{$A+, D-, L-, S-, R-}
```

Programmers seeking better performance should include the compiler directive just listed. The directive word-aligns constants and variables for 80x86 machines, removes debugger overhead, and disables stack and range checking.

Parameter Directives

In the same way that a QuickPascal switch directive instructs the QuickPascal compiler to enable or disable specific processing, QuickPascal parameter directives require your program to provide a value (parameter) that the compiler uses during compilation. QuickPascal provides several parameter directives.

The {$I *filename*} directive tells QuickPascal to include the specified source file at the location of the directive. Prior to the development of units, Pascal programmers placed commonly used functions and procedures in a source file they could later include in their programs. When QuickPascal encounters the {$I *filename*} directive, QuickPascal searches for the include file in the directory specified in the file's pathname and, if necessary, in the paths defined in the QuickPascal Options menu's Environment option. The larger the include file, the longer the program takes to compile; therefore, most newer programs use QuickPascal units. If the include filename does not specify an extension, QuickPascal assumes INC.

The {$L *objectFile*} compiler directive tells QuickPascal to link the specified object file with the current program. The object file is created by an assembler. Within your program, you must specify the assembly-language routine as EXTERNAL.

```
PROCEDURE Some_Routine(x, y, z: Byte); EXTERNAL;
FUNCTION Some_Function(a, b): Integer; EXTERNAL;
```

When QuickPascal encounters the {$L *objectFile*} directive, it searches for the object file in the directory specified in the file's pathname and, if necessary, in the paths defined in the QuickPascal Options menu's Environment option.

The {$M *stackSize*, *minimumHeap*, *maximumHeap*} compiler directive controls the amount of memory allocated for the stack and the heap. QuickPascal uses the stack to store local variables during procedure and function calls. All routines that allocate memory dynamically use the heap. By default, QuickPascal uses the setting {$M 16384, 0, 655360}. Most programs won't modify these values; however, if you are writing a memory-resident TSR program, you will want to reduce the amount of allocated but unused memory by using this directive. And if your program consumes all available space, this directive lets your program request more space.

CONDITIONAL COMPILATION

Often you want your program to perform one set of statements when some condition is met and another set when the condition fails. The same can hold true for compilation. The QuickPascal compiler switch directive {$N+} directs QuickPascal to generate code statements that use the 80x87 math coprocessor. When your program contains the {$N+} directive, it will execute faster on computers with a math coprocessor. However, the program will not execute at all on a system without a math coprocessor. By using QuickPascal's conditional compilation capabilities, your program can test during compilation whether the system has a math coprocessor. If so, the program can include the {$N+} compiler directive. If the system does not have a math coprocessor, the compiler directive won't be included. The executable program will always work on the system on which it was compiled. If you move the program to a new computer, however, you will need to recompile. During compilation, QuickPascal will test the new system for a math coprocessor and generate code accordingly.

During compilation, QuickPascal defines several symbols that your programs can test using conditional compilation. The following table describes each predefined symbol.

Symbol	Description
VER10	Defined for QuickPascal version 1.0
MSDOS	Defined for MS-DOS
CPU86	Defined for a processor in the 80x86 family
CPU87	Defined if an 80x87 math coprocessor is present at compilation time

The {$IFDEF *symbol*} compiler directive tells QuickPascal to test whether the specified symbol is defined. If it is, the compiler compiles the statements that follow the directive until it encounters an {$ENDIF} or an {$ELSE} directive. For example, the following directives test for the existence of an 80x87 math coprocessor and set the {$N} compiler directive accordingly.

```
{$IFDEF CPU87}
{$N+} { provide math-coprocessor support }
{$ELSE}
{$N-} { no math coprocessor }
{$ENDIF}
```

QuickPascal also provides the {$IFNDEF *symbol*} directive, the opposite of {$IFDEF *symbol*}. With {$IFNDEF}, QuickPascal compiles the statements that follow only if the specified symbol has not been defined.

The {$IFOPT *option*} directive tells QuickPascal to include the statements that follow only if the specified compiler switch is in effect. For example, the following directives test whether the compiler is placing debug information in the executable file. If so, the program displays a warning message.

```
{$IFOPT D+}
Writeln('Program contains debugger information.');
Writeln('For better performance, recompile with');
Writeln('{$D-}.');
{$ENDIF}
```

In addition to the predefined symbols, QuickPascal lets your program define its own symbols using the {$DEFINE *symbol*} compiler directive. For example, the following directive defines the symbol TESTING that indicates you are still testing the application:

```
{$DEFINE TESTING}
```

If you place this directive at the top of your program, you can use it throughout your program for conditional compilation. For example, the following directives test whether the symbol TESTING is defined. If so, the program enables debug information and range and stack checking. If not, the program disables debug and run-time checking in order to improve performance.

```
{$IFDEF TESTING}
{$D+, L+, R+, S+}
{$ELSE}
{$D-, L-, R-, S-}
{$ENDIF}
```

Finally, the {$UNDEF *symbol*} compiler directive undefines a conditional-compilation symbol. Assume, for example, that you have included debug Writeln statements in several procedures and functions. Using conditional compilation, you can enable and disable the statements as shown here:

```
{$IFDEF DEBUGLINE}
Writeln('Debug information');
{$ENDIF}
```

In some cases you might want to disable the debug Writeln statements for a procedure you know is working. To do so, you can undefine the DEBUGGING symbol before the procedure and then redefine the symbol after the procedure as shown here:

```
{$UNDEF DEBUGGING}
PROCEDURE Test;
BEGIN
  {$IFDEF DEBUGGING}
  Writeln('Debug information');
  {$ENDIF}
END;
{$DEFINE DEBUGGING}
```

By enabling and disabling the debug Writeln statements in this way, you avoid having to remove the statements from your program until you're sure you no longer need them.

The QuickPascal conditional-compilation directives increase your programming flexibility. Experiment with the directives and you will find them to be quite useful.

PART III
QuickPascal Functions and Procedures

The entries in this alphabetic reference section describe each Microsoft QuickPascal function and procedure. Each entry includes the name of the unit in which the function or procedure is located, a brief description of the function or procedure's purpose, its syntax, a list of arguments, notes about use, and references to related functions and procedures. Most entries also include sample programs that illustrate the use of the functions and procedures.

The Index to Functions and Procedures by Unit at the end of this section lists Microsoft QuickPascal functions and procedures alphabetically within their units.

Abs   System

Returns an expression's absolute value.

Syntax
FUNCTION Abs(*value*:<*integer or real type*>):
  <*same type as argument*>;

Arguments
value is the expression for which Abs returns the absolute value.

Notes

An expression's absolute value is the expression's value without a sign.

Example

```
PROGRAM AbsoluteValue;

BEGIN
  Writeln('Absolute value of -5 is ', Abs(-5));
  Writeln('Absolute value of 5 is ', Abs(5));
  Writeln('Absolute value of -4 * 4 is ',
    Abs(-4 * 4));
  Writeln('Absolute value of 100 - 200 is ',
    Abs(100 - 200));
END.
```

Related routines: Frac, Int, Odd, Random, Randomize, Round, Sqr, Sqrt, Trunc

Addr
System

Returns the 32-bit address of a variable, function, or procedure.

Syntax

FUNCTION Addr(VAR *identifier*: *<any type>*): Pointer;

Arguments

identifier is the name of the variable, function, or procedure for which Addr returns the 32-bit address.

Notes

The 32-bit address contains a 16-bit segment and a 16-bit offset address.

After your program uses Addr to assign an address value to a pointer, your program can reference the value stored at the address using the caret (^).

The Addr function returns the same result as the @ operator.

Example

```
PROGRAM AddExitProcedure;

USES
  Crt;  { contains ClrScr procedure }

VAR
  defaultExitProc: Pointer;

{ declare the exit procedure }
{$F+}  { create code for a FAR call to procedure }
PROCEDURE EndMessage;
{$F-}  { restore near call processing }
BEGIN
  { restore the original exit procedure }
  ExitProc := defaultExitProc;
  ClrScr;
  Writeln('Processing complete');
END;
BEGIN
  { save the original exit procedure }
  defaultExitProc := ExitProc;

  { assign the procedure address to
    the global variable ExitProc }
  ExitProc := @EndMessage;

  Writeln('About to end program; ',
    press Enter to continue.');
  Readln;
END.
```

Related routines: CSeg, DSeg, New, Ofs, Ptr, Seg, SPtr, SSeg

Append   System

Opens an existing text file for output, advancing the file pointer to the end of the file in order to append new text.

Syntax
PROCEDURE Append(VAR *filePointer*: Text);

Arguments

filePointer is a file pointer of type Text with which your program has associated a filename using Assign.

Notes

If the specified file doesn't already exist on disk, a run-time error will occur. To check for this error, disable I/O checking with the {$I-} compiler directive and test IOResult.

Append works only for text files. To append output to a typed or untyped file, open the file using Reset and then move the file pointer to the end of the file using Seek.

If the specified file is already open, Append closes the file and opens it in append mode.

Example

```
PROGRAM AppendFile;

VAR
  InputFile: Text;       { pointer to input file }
  OutputFile: Text;      { pointer to output file }
  Line: STRING;          { line of text from file }
  SourceBuffer: ARRAY[1..4096] OF Char;
  TargetBuffer: ARRAY[1..4096] OF Char;

BEGIN
  { assign input filename to file pointer }
  Assign(InputFile, 'APPEND.NEW');

  {$I-}   { disable I/O checking }
  Reset(InputFile);              { prepare for input }
  {$I+}   { enable I/O checking }

  IF (IOResult <> 0) THEN
    Writeln('Unable to open APPEND.NEW')
  ELSE
    BEGIN
      { assign output filename to file pointer }
      Assign(OutputFile, 'APPEND.OLD');
```

```
    {$I-}  { disable I/O checking }
    Append(OutputFile);   { prepare for output }
    {$I+}  { enable I/O checking }
    IF (IOResult <> 0) THEN
      Writeln('Unable to open APPEND.OLD')
    ELSE
      BEGIN
        { assign new file buffers }
        SetTextBuf(InputFile, SourceBuffer,
          SizeOf(SourceBuffer));
        SetTextBuf(OutputFile, TargetBuffer,
          SizeOf(TargetBuffer));

        { copy all characters in the file }
        WHILE (NOT Eof(InputFile)) DO
          BEGIN
            Readln(InputFile, Line);
            Writeln(OutputFile, Line);
          END;
        Close(InputFile);
        Close(OutputFile);
      END;
  END;
END.
```

Related routines: Assign, AssignCrt, Close, Eof, IOResult, Reset, Rewrite, Seek, Write, Writeln

_Arc MSGraph

Draws an elliptical arc in graphics mode.

Syntax
PROCEDURE _Arc(*upperLeft*, *upperLefty*, *lowerRightx*, *lowerRighty*, *startx*, *starty*, *stopx*, *stopy*: Integer);

Arguments
upperLeft and *upperLefty* are the *x* and *y* viewport coordinates of the upper left corner of the rectangle that bounds the ellipse.

lowerRightx and *lowerRighty* are the *x* and *y* viewport coordinates of the lower right corner of the rectangle that bounds the ellipse.

startx and *starty* are the *x* and *y* viewport coordinates of the arc's start vector.

stopx and *stopy* are the *x* and *y* viewport coordinates of the arc's stop vector.

Notes

_Arc draws an arc using logical screen (that is, viewport) coordinates.

The rectangle that bounds the ellipse defines the ellipse's shape and size. The arc is drawn along the ellipse counterclockwise from its start vector to its stop vector. The vector coordinates define lines from the center of the arc through the ellipse. The intersections of the lines and the ellipse mark the start and stop points.

Upon _Arc's completion, your program can invoke the _GrStatus function to test for the following status values:

Status	Meaning
_GrClipped	Arc clipped to fit viewport
_GrInvalidParameter	Invalid argument in call to _Arc
_GrNoOutput	No image drawn
_GrNotInProperMode	Invalid video display mode

Example

```
PROGRAM Arcs;
USES
  MSGraph,  { contains graphics routines }
  Crt;      { contains the KeyPressed function }

VAR
  status: Integer;  { status of function call }

BEGIN
  { set the video mode to 320 by 200 graphics }
  status := _SetVideoMode(_MRes4Color);

  _Arc(55, 20, 130, 150, 50, 150, 160, 80);
```

```
_Arc(180, 50, 280, 150, 130, 35, 230, 100);

_SetTextPosition(23, 8);
_OutText('Press any key to continue');

WHILE (NOT KeyPressed) DO
   ;

{ restore the original video mode }
status := _SetVideoMode(_DefaultMode);
END.
```

Related routines: _Arc_wxy, _Ellipse, _GrStatus, _SetColor

_Arc_wxy   MSGraph

Draws an elliptical arc in graphics mode, using window coordinates.

Syntax
PROCEDURE _Arc_wxy(VAR *upperLefty, lowerRightxy, startxy, stopxy*: _WXYCoord);

Arguments
upperLefty is a record of type _WXYCoord that contains the *x* and *y* window coordinates of the upper left corner of the rectangle that bounds the ellipse.

lowerRightxy is a record of type _WXYCoord that contains the *x* and *y* window coordinates of the lower right corner of the rectangle that bounds the ellipse.

startxy is a record of type _WXYCoord that contains the *x* and *y* window coordinates of the arc's start vector.

stopxy is a record of type _WXYCoord that contains the *x* and *y* window coordinates of the arc's stop vector.

Notes
_Arc_wxy draws an ellipse, using window coordinates defined by _SetWindow.

The MSGraph unit defines the record type _WXYCoord as follows:

```
_WXYCoord = RECORD
  wx: Double;   { window x coordinate }
  wy: Double;   { window y coordinate }
END;
```

With the exception that it uses window coordinates, _Arc_wxy behaves in the same way as _Arc.

Example

```
PROGRAM Arcwxy;

USES
  MSGraph,   { contains graphics routines }
  Crt;       { contains the KeyPressed function }

VAR
  status: Integer;
  topLeft: _WXYCoord;
  bottomRight: _WXYCoord;
  start, stop: _WXYCoord;

BEGIN
  { set the video mode to 320 by 200 graphics }
  status := _SetVideoMode(_MRes4Color);

  _SetWindow(False, 0.0, 0.0, 100.0, 100.0);

  topLeft.wx := 20.0;       topLeft.wy := 20.0;
  bottomRight.wx := 80.0;   bottomRight.wy := 80.0;
  start.wx := 0.0;          start.wy := 0.0;
  stop.wx := 100.0;         stop.wy := 0.0;

  _Arc_wxy(topLeft, bottomRight, start, stop);

  _SetTextPosition(23, 8);
  _OutText('Press any key to continue');

  WHILE (NOT KeyPressed) DO
    ;

  { restore the original video mode }
  status := _SetVideoMode(_DefaultMode);
END.
```

Related routines: _Arc, _Ellipse, _GrStatus, _SetColor, _SetWindow

ArcTan
System

Calculates the arctangent of a value in radians.

Syntax
FUNCTION ArcTan(*tangentValue*: <*real type*>):
  <*real type*>;

Arguments
tangentValue is the value for which ArcTan returns the arctangent.

Notes
The tangent of an angle is a number. The arctangent of that number is the normalized angle in radians.

Example
```
PROGRAM ArcTangent;

BEGIN
  { use Alt+227 to create π }
  Writeln('ArcTan of π is ', ArcTan(Pi));
  Writeln('ArcTan of 2π is ', ArcTan(2 * Pi));
END.
```

Related routines: Cos, Pi, Sin

Assign
System

Associates a file pointer with a filename.

Syntax
PROCEDURE Assign(VAR *filePointer*: <*file type*>;
  filename: <*string type*>);

Arguments

filePointer is a file pointer to an unopened typed, untyped, or text file.

filename is a character string containing a maximum of 79 characters (DOS pathnames cannot exceed 64 characters) that contains the name of the file or hardware device to which the file pointer will refer.

Notes

The filename can contain a complete DOS pathname with a disk-drive letter followed by subdirectories. If the filename contains only an empty string, Assign prepares the file for DOS I/O redirection.

The Assign procedure does not test whether the specified file exists because Assign does not yet know whether your program will use the file pointer for read, write, or append operations.

If the file referenced by the pointer your program passes to Assign is open, the previous assignment is lost.

Example
See Append.

Related routines: Append, AssignCrt, Close, IOResult, Reset, Rewrite

AssignCrt   Crt

Assigns a text file pointer to the console device.

Syntax
PROCEDURE AssignCrt(VAR *filePointer*: Text);

Arguments

filePointer is a file pointer of type Text that will be assigned to the keyboard or the screen display.

Notes

The AssignCrt procedure lets your program perform screen output faster than standard DOS file operations will. The Crt unit provides direct access to the BIOS or Crt controller, bypassing DOS, thereby increasing performance.

Example

```
PROGRAM CantRedirect;

USES
  Crt;   { contains AssignCrt procedure }

VAR
  outputText: Text;

BEGIN
  Assign(Output, '');  { allow output redirection }
  Rewrite(Output);
  AssignCrt(outputText);
  Rewrite(outputText);
  Writeln(outputText,
    'Cannot redirect this message');
  Writeln('This message is redirectable');
END.
```

Related routines: Append, Assign, Close, IOResult, Reset, Rewrite, Writeln

BlockRead   System

Reads data from an untyped file into a program-defined memory buffer.

Syntax

PROCEDURE BlockRead(VAR *filePointer*: FILE;
   VAR *buffer*: <any type>; *blockCount*: Word
   [; VAR *actualCount*: Word]);

Arguments

filePointer is a file pointer to the untyped file to be read.

buffer is a variable of any type into which the file data is to be read. The default block size is 128 bytes. The variable must be large enough to store an entire block.

blockCount specifies the number of blocks to be read from the file.

actualCount is an optional argument that contains the number of blocks actually read from the file.

Notes

Your program can specify the file's block size when it uses Reset to open the file. The default block size is 128 bytes. The maximum buffer size is 64 KB.

The BlockRead procedure does not perform range checking to ensure that the data will fit into the specified buffer.

If the file size is not an integer multiple of the block size, a portion of the file might be left unread.

Example

```
PROGRAM BinCopy;

VAR
  inputFile: FILE;       { pointer to input file }
  outputFile: FILE;      { pointer to output file }
  sourceFile: STRING;    { filename to copy }
  targetFile: STRING;    { target filename }
  buffer: ARRAY[1..4096] OF Char;  { I/O buffer }
  bytesRead: Word;       { number of bytes read }
  bytesWritten: Word;    { number of bytes written }

BEGIN
  { get source filename }
  IF (ParamCount > 0) THEN
    sourceFile := ParamStr(1)
  ELSE
    BEGIN
      { get the filename from the user }
      Write('Enter name of source file: ');
      Readln(sourceFile);
    END;
  { get target filename }
  IF (ParamCount > 1) THEN
    targetFile := ParamStr(2)
```

```
ELSE
  BEGIN
    { get the filename from the user }
    Write('Enter name of target file: ');
    Readln(targetFile);
  END;

{ assign input filename to file pointer }
Assign(inputFile, sourceFile);

{$I-}   { disable I/O checking }
Reset(inputFile, 1);       { block size of 1 }
{$I+}   { enable I/O checking }
IF (IOResult <> 0) THEN
  Writeln('Unable to open file: ', sourceFile)
ELSE
  BEGIN
    { assign output filename to file pointer }
    Assign(outputFile, targetFile);
    {$I-}   { disable I/O checking }
    Rewrite(outputFile, 1);   { block size of 1 }
    {$I+}   { enable I/O checking }

    IF (IOResult <> 0) THEN
      Writeln('Unable to open the file: ',
        targetFile)
    ELSE
      BEGIN
        { copy all characters in the file }
        REPEAT
          BlockRead(inputFile, buffer,
            SizeOf(buffer), bytesRead);
          BlockWrite(outputFile, buffer,
            bytesRead, bytesWritten);
        UNTIL (bytesRead = 0) OR
          (bytesRead <> bytesWritten);
        Close(inputFile);
        Close(outputFile);
      END;
  END;
END.
```

Related routines: Append, Assign, BlockWrite, FileSize, IOResult, Reset

BlockWrite — System

Writes data from a program-defined data buffer to an untyped file.

Syntax
PROCEDURE BlockWrite(VAR *filePointer*: FILE;
 VAR *buffer*: <any type>; *blockCount*: Word
 [; VAR *actualCount*: Word]);

Arguments
filePointer is a file pointer to an untyped file into which BlockWrite writes the data.

buffer is a variable of any type containing the data that BlockWrite is to write to the file.

blockCount specifies the number of blocks to be written to the file.

actualCount is an optional argument that returns the number of blocks actually written to the file.

Notes
By default, BlockWrite uses a block size of 128 bytes. Your program can change the block size when it uses Rewrite to open the file. The maximum buffer size is 64 KB.

Example
See BlockRead.

Related routines: Append, Assign, BlockRead, FileSize, IOResult, Rewrite

ChDir — System

Changes the current directory, the current or disk drive, or both.

Syntax

PROCEDURE ChDir(*path*: <*string type*>);

Arguments

path is a character string containing the DOS pathname of the desired subdirectory.

Notes

If the specified subdirectory does not exist, a run-time error occurs and the program stops. By disabling I/O checking using the {$I–} compiler directive and testing IOResult, your program can test for and detect nonexistent subdirectories.

If the DOS pathname specifies a disk-drive letter, ChDir selects the specified drive as the default drive.

Example

```
PROGRAM ChangeDirectory;

VAR
  directory: STRING;

BEGIN
  Write('Type in name of desired directory: ');
  Readln(directory);

  { disable I/O checking }
  {$I-}
  { select the desired directory }
  ChDir(directory);
  { enable I/O checking }
  {$I+}

  { test status of directory selection }
  IF (IOResult <> 0) THEN
    Writeln('Directory does not exist: ',
      directory);
END.
```

Related routines: GetDir, IOResult, MkDir, RmDir

Chr — System

Returns the ASCII character that corresponds to a numeric value.

Syntax
FUNCTION Chr(*value*: Byte): Char;

Arguments
value is the ASCII code number (from 0 through 255) of the character.

Notes
The Chr and Ord functions perform inverse tasks. Chr converts a numeric value to an ASCII character, and Ord converts an ASCII character to its numeric representation.

Example
```
PROGRAM ChrTest;

VAR
  value: Integer;

BEGIN
  FOR value := 33 TO 255 DO
    Writeln('Value: ', value:4,
        ' Character: ', Chr(value));
END.
```

Related routines: Length, Ord, UpCase

_ClearScreen — MSGraph

Erases the contents of either the screen, the text window, or the graphics viewport.

Syntax
PROCEDURE _ClearScreen(*screenRegion*: Integer);

Arguments

screenRegion defines the area of the screen to be erased. The MSGraph unit defines the following region constants:

Constant	Screen Area
_GClearScreen	Entire screen display
_GWindow	Text window
_GViewport	Graphics viewport

Notes

_ClearScreen clears the specified area and fills it with the current background color.

Upon completion of the _ClearScreen procedure, your program can test the return value of _GrStatus to determine _ClearScreen's success.

Status	Meaning
_GrInvalidParameter	Invalid argument in call to _ClearScreen
_GrNotInProperMode	Invalid video display mode

Example

```
PROGRAM ClearScreenTest;

USES
  MSGraph;   { contains _ClearScreen procedure }

BEGIN

  _ClearScreen(_GClearScreen);
  Writeln('Text now appears in home position');
END.
```

Related routines: _GetBkColor, _SetBkColor, _GrStatus, _SetTextWindow, _SetViewport

Close   System

Closes a file and updates the file's directory entry if necessary.

Syntax
PROCEDURE Close(VAR *filePointer*: <*file type*>);

Arguments
filePointer is a file pointer to a typed, untyped, or text file that Assign associates with a specific file.

Notes
Close flushes all file buffers and updates the directory entries for a file opened for output.

By default, QuickPascal automatically closes all open files when your program completes execution.

Example
See Append.

Related routines: Append, Assign, AssignCrt, Reset, Rewrite

ClrEol
Crt

Clears the current line from the cursor position to the end of the line.

Syntax
PROCEDURE ClrEol;

Arguments
None.

Notes
ClrEol clears the line by assigning a blank character to each character position. The text attribute for the blank characters depends upon the current background color.

Upon completion of the ClrEol procedure, the cursor remains at its original position.

Example

```
PROGRAM ClrEolTest;

USES
  Crt;  { contains ClrEol, ClrScr, and GotoXY }

VAR
  names: ARRAY[1..5] OF STRING;
  index: Byte;      { index into the array }

BEGIN
  ClrScr;  { erase the screen display }

  Write('Enter name: ');

  FOR index := 1 TO 5 DO
    BEGIN
      GotoXY(13, 1);
      ClrEol;              { erase the previous entry }
      Readln(names[index]);
    END;

  Writeln;

  FOR index := 1 TO 5 DO
    Writeln(names[index]);
END.
```

Related routines: ClrScr, DelLine, GotoXY, InsLine, TextBackground, WhereX, WhereY, Window

ClrScr   Crt

Erases the contents of the screen display.

Syntax
PROCEDURE ClrScr;

Arguments
None.

Notes

The ClrScr procedure clears the text window and assigns the background color to it. Upon completion, ClrScr places the cursor at the upper left corner of the window.

Programs that create graphics using the MSGraph unit use the _ClearScreen procedure; otherwise, most programs use the ClrScr procedure.

Example
See ClrEol.

Related routines: ClrEol, DelLine, GotoXY, InsLine, TextBackground, WhereX, WhereY, Window

Concat
System

Concatenates, or joins together, two or more strings.

Syntax
FUNCTION Concat(*str1* [, *str2*...]: <*string type*>): <*string type*>;

Arguments
str1 is the first character string to concatenate. To join several strings together, separate the strings with commas. Concat joins the strings from left to right.

Notes
The largest character string Concat returns is 255 characters long. If the number of characters in the concatenated string exceeds 255, Concat truncates it.

The QuickPascal plus operator also lets your program concatenate strings.

```
strResult := str1 + str2 + str3;
```

Example

```
PROGRAM Concatenate;

VAR
  language: STRING;
  book: STRING;
  result: STRING;

BEGIN
  language := 'Microsoft QuickPascal ';
  book := 'Programmer''s Quick Reference';

  Result := Concat('Language: ', language,
    'Book: ', book);
    Writeln(Result);
END.
```

Related routines: Copy, Delete, Insert, Length, Pos, Str, Val

Copy   System

Copies a substring from a string.

Syntax
FUNCTION Copy(*sourceStr*: <*string type*>; *startIndex*, *numChar*: <*integer type*>): <*string type*>;

Arguments
sourceStr is the string from which the substring is copied.

startIndex is the index of the first character in the substring.

numChar is the number of characters in the substring.

Notes
If *startIndex* is greater than the length of the string, Copy returns an empty string.

If *numChar* exceeds the number of characters remaining in the string, Copy returns characters only up through the last character in the string.

Example

```
PROGRAM CopyName;

VAR
  name: STRING;          { name to copy }
  firstName: STRING;     { first name }
  lastName: STRING;      { last name }
  wholeName: STRING;     { copy of the entire name }

BEGIN
  name := 'William Gates';

  { assign the first name, characters 1 through 7 }
    firstName := Copy(Name, 1, 7);

  { assign the last name, characters 9 through 13 }
  lastName := Copy(Name, 9, 5);

  { assign the entire name }
  wholeName := Name;

  Writeln('Name: ', name);
  Writeln('First name: ', firstName);
  Writeln('Last name: ', lastName);
  Writeln('Whole name: ', wholeName);
END.
```

Related routines: Concat, Delete, Insert, Length, Pos, Str, Val

Cos
System

Returns the cosine of an angle.

Syntax
FUNCTION Cos(*angle*: <*real type*>): <*real type*>;

Arguments
angle is an angle expressed in radians.

Notes

The angle your program passes to Cos must be in radians. To convert degrees to radians, use the following equation:

Radians = Degrees / 180.0 ∗ π

Example

```
PROGRAM Cosine;

BEGIN
  { use Alt+227 to create π }
  Writeln('Cosine of π is ', Cos(Pi));
  Writeln('Cosine of 2π is ', Cos(2 * Pi));
END.
```

Related routines: ArcTan, Pi, Sin

CSeg
System

Returns the value of the code segment register.

Syntax
FUNCTION CSeg: Word;

Arguments
None.

Notes
The code segment register stores the 16-bit code segment address. The code segment holds your program as well as executable functions and procedures.

Example

```
PROGRAM SegmentInfo;

BEGIN
  Writeln('Segment Information');
  Writeln('CSEG: ', CSeg);
  Writeln('DSEG: ', DSeg);
  Writeln('SSEG: ', SSeg);
  Writeln('SPTR: ', SPtr);
END.
```

Related routines: Addr, DSeg, Ofs, Ptr, Seg, SPtr, SSeg

Dec   System

Decrements an ordinal variable by the specified amount.

Syntax
PROCEDURE Dec(VAR *ordinalVariable*: <*ordinal type*>
  [; *decrement*: LongInt]);

Arguments
ordinalVariable is the ordinal variable to be decremented.

decrement is the optional amount to subtract from the ordinal variable. If you don't specify *decrement*, the default is 1.

Notes
Ordinal types include Boolean, Char, integer types, and subrange and enumerated types.

Decrementing an ordinal variable by 1 is functionally equivalent to using the Pred function.

If your program decrements past the first value in an ordinal type, a range error occurs. Using the {$R+} compiler directive, your program can test for this error.

Example
```
PROGRAM DecInc;

VAR
  value: Integer;

BEGIN
  value := 1024;

  WHILE (value > 0) DO
    BEGIN
      Writeln(value);
      Dec(value, 64);
    END;
```

```
  WHILE (value <= 4096) DO
    BEGIN
      Writeln(value);
      Inc(value, 1024);
    END;
END.
```

Related routines: First, Inc, Last, Ord, Pred, Succ

Delay   Crt

Temporarily suspends program execution for the specified number of milliseconds.

Syntax
PROCEDURE Delay(*milliseconds*: Word);

Arguments
milliseconds specifies the number of milliseconds to delay, from 0 through 65,535.

Notes
1000 milliseconds equal 1 second.

Example
```
PROGRAM MakeSound;

USES
  Crt;    { contains Sound and NoSound procedures }

VAR
  frequency: Word;

BEGIN

  FOR frequency := 1500 DOWNTO 800 DO
    BEGIN
      Sound(frequency); { produce the sound }
      Delay(10);        { delay 10 milliseconds }
    END;
```

(continued)

continued

```
  NoSound;                  { turn off the last sound }
END.
```

Related routines: KeyPressed, NoSound, ReadKey, Sound

Delete — System

Removes a substring from a string.

Syntax
PROCEDURE Delete(VAR *sourceStr*: <*string type*>;
  startIndex, *numChar*: <*integer type*>);

Arguments
sourceStr is the character string to be modified.

startIndex is the index to the first character of the substring to be deleted.

numChar is the number of characters in the substring.

Notes
If the starting index is greater than the number of characters in the string, Delete leaves the string unchanged.

If the number of characters to delete exceeds the number of characters in the string, Delete removes characters only through the end of the string.

Example
```
PROGRAM DeleteCharacters;

VAR
  originalString: STRING;
  result: STRING;

BEGIN
  originalString := '123456789';
```

```
{ delete the characters 4, 5, and 6 }
result := originalString;
Delete(result, 4, 3);
Writeln(originalString,
   ' minus 4, 5, and 6 is ', result);

{ delete the character 1 }
result := originalString;
Delete(result, 1, 1);
Writeln(originalString,
   ' minus 1 is ', result);

{ delete the characters 8 and 9 }
result := originalString;
Delete(result, 8, 2);
Writeln(originalString,
   ' minus 8 and 9 is ', result);
END.
```

Related routines: Concat, Copy, Insert, Length, Pos, Str, Val

DelLine   Crt

Deletes from the text window the line currently containing the cursor, scrolling all lines below up one position.

Syntax
PROCEDURE DelLine;

Arguments
None.

Notes
After your program deletes a line, the line cannot be recovered.

When DelLine removes the line and scrolls others up, DelLine adds a new line at the bottom of the window. The new line uses the current text background color.

Example

```pascal
PROGRAM DeleteLine;

USES
  Crt;

VAR
  lineNumber: Byte;  { current line number }
  count: Byte;       { loop counter }
BEGIN
  ClrScr;
  Window(20, 10, 60, 20);
  FOR lineNumber := 1 TO 10 DO
    BEGIN
      FOR count := 1 TO 10 DO
        Write(lineNumber:3);
      Writeln;
    END;

  GotoXY(1, 5);   { delete line 5 }
  Delay(5000);    { pause to display line 5 }
  DelLine;
  Delay(5000);    { delay to note line gone }
END.
```

Related routines: ClrEol, ClrScr, GotoXY, InsLine, TextBackground, WhereX, WhereY, Window

DiskFree

Dos

Returns the number of bytes available on the disk in the specified drive.

Syntax
FUNCTION DiskFree(*drive*: Byte): LongInt;

Arguments
drive is the number (from 0 through 26) of the desired disk drive.

Notes

Drive 0 is the current drive, 1 is drive A, 2 is drive B, 3 is drive C, and so on.

If the specified disk-drive number is invalid, DiskFree returns the value −1.

Example

```
PROGRAM DiskSpace;

USES
  Dos;                { contains DiskFree function }

VAR
  freeSpace: LongInt;

BEGIN
  freeSpace := DiskFree(0);  { 0 is current drive }
  Writeln('Amount of unused disk space: ',
    freeSpace, ' bytes');
END.
```

Related routine: DiskSize

DiskSize

Dos

Returns a disk drive's total storage capacity (used and unused).

Syntax
FUNCTION DiskSize(*drive*: Byte): LongInt;

Arguments

drive is the number (from 0 through 26) of the desired disk drive.

Notes

Drive 0 is the current drive, 1 is drive A, 2 is drive B, 3 is drive C, and so on.

If the specified disk-drive number is invalid, DiskSize returns the value −1.

Example

```
PROGRAM ShowDiskSize;

USES
  Dos;                    { contains DiskSize function }

VAR
  size: LongInt;

BEGIN
  size := DiskSize(0);  { get the disk size }

  Writeln('Size of current disk: ',
    size, ' bytes');
END.
```

Related routine: DiskFree

_DisplayCursor   MSGraph

Enables or disables the cursor.

Syntax
FUNCTION _DisplayCursor(*state*: Boolean): Boolean;

Arguments
state is a true-or-false value that tells _DisplayCursor to turn the cursor on (true) or off (false).

Notes
In text mode the cursor is on by default. In graphics mode the cursor is off by default. Each time _DisplayCursor completes execution, it returns the previous setting.

Example

```
PROGRAM DisplayGraphicsCursor;

USES
  MSGraph,   { contains graphics routines }
  Crt;       { contains ReadKey function }
```

```pascal
VAR
  status: Integer;    { function return status }
  response: Char;     { user response }
  oldCursor: Boolean; { previous setting }
  str: STRING;        { buffer for _OutText }

BEGIN
  status := _SetVideoMode(_MRes4Color);

  { draw a rectangle on the screen }
  _Rectangle(_GBorder, 50, 50, 200, 150);

  _SetTextPosition(22, 8);
  _OutText('Fill box (Y/N)? ');

  oldCursor := _DisplayCursor(True);

  REPEAT
    response := ReadKey;
    IF (response IN ['y', 'Y', 'N', 'n']) THEN
      BEGIN
        str[1] := response;
        str[0] := Chr(1);
        _OutText(str);
        response := UpCase(response);
      END;
  UNTIL (response IN ['N', 'Y']);

  IF (response = 'Y') THEN
    _FloodFill(100, 100, _GetColor);

  oldCursor := _DisplayCursor(False);
  { pause for the user to press a key }
  _SetTextPosition(22, 8);
  _OutText('Press any key to continue');
  response := ReadKey;

  { restore video mode }
  status := _SetVideoMode(_DefaultMode);
END.
```

Related routines: _GetTextCursor, _SetTextCursor

Dispose

System

Deallocates memory previously allocated for a dynamic variable.

Syntax
PROCEDURE Dispose(VAR *pointerVariable*: Pointer);

Arguments
pointerVariable is a pointer to memory previously allocated from the heap by the New function.

Notes
Do not mix memory-allocation methods by combining calls to New and Dispose with calls to GetMem and FreeMem. Doing so makes your program difficult to understand.

By default, if the memory location your program passes to Dispose does not point to a dynamic variable in the heap, a run-time error results.

Example
```
PROGRAM DynamicMemory;

TYPE
  bigArray = ARRAY[1..2000] OF Integer;

VAR
  arrayPtr: ^bigArray;   { pointer to an array }
  index: Integer;        { array index }

BEGIN
  IF (MaxAvail < SizeOf(bigArray)) THEN
    Writeln('Insufficient heap space available')
  ELSE
    BEGIN
      { allocate memory for the array }
      New(arrayPtr);
```

```
        FOR index := 1 TO 2000 DO
          arrayPtr^[index] := Index;
        FOR index := 1 TO 2000 DO
          Writeln(arrayPtr^[index]);

        Dispose(arrayPtr);
     END;
END.
```

Related routines: Addr, FreeMem, GetMem, Mark, MaxAvail, MemAvail, New, Release, SizeOf

DosExitCode   Dos

Returns the exit status code of a terminated child process.

Syntax
FUNCTION DosExitCode: Word;

Arguments
None.

Notes
The QuickPascal Exec procedure lets your program invoke a child process. The DosExitCode function returns the exit status of the child process code. The program run as a child process defines the meaning of the exit status code.

The low byte of the return value contains the exit code. The high byte contains one of the following values indicating how the program terminated:

Value	Termination Condition
0	Normal termination
1	Ctrl+Break termination
2	Device-error termination
3	Memory-resident termination using Keep

Example

```
{$M 16384, 0, 65536}   { reduce stack and heap }
PROGRAM DOSExitTest;

USES
  Dos;

BEGIN
  { prevent child process from
    changing interrupt vectors }
  SwapVectors;
  Exec('C:\COMMAND.COM', '/C DIR');
  { restore interrupt vectors }
  SwapVectors;
  Writeln('Exit code: ', DosExitCode);
END.
```

Related routines: Exec, Exit, Halt, Hi, Keep, Lo, RunError

DosVersion   Dos

Returns the operating-system version number.

Syntax
FUNCTION DosVersion: Word;

Arguments
None.

Notes
DosVersion places the major version number in the low byte of the return value and the minor version number in the high byte.

Example

```
PROGRAM DisplayDOSVersion;

USES
  Dos;    { contains the DosVersion function }
```

```
VAR
  version: Integer;

BEGIN
  version := DosVersion;
  Writeln('Current DOS version:', Lo(version):2,
    '.', Hi(version));
END.
```

Related routines: Hi, Lo, Swap

DSeg System

Returns the value of the data segment register.

Syntax
FUNCTION DSeg: Word;

Arguments
None.

Notes
The data segment register stores the 16-bit data segment address. The data segment holds your program and unit global variables.

Example
See CSeg.

Related routines: Addr, CSeg, Ofs, Ptr, Seg, SPtr, SSeg

_Ellipse MSGraph

Draws an ellipse in graphics mode.

Syntax

PROCEDURE _Ellipse(*fillControl*, *upperLeftx*, *upperLefty*, *lowerRightx*, *lowerRighty*: Integer);

Arguments

fillControl specifies whether _Ellipse fills the ellipse using the current color and fill pattern or simply draws the ellipse border. The MSGraph unit defines two constants for fill control.

Constant	Meaning
_GFillInterior	Fill the ellipse
_GBorder	Draw the ellipse border only

upperLeftx and *upperLefty* are the *x* and *y* viewport coordinates of the upper left corner of the rectangle that bounds the ellipse.

lowerRightx and *lowerRighty* are the *x* and *y* viewport coordinates of the lower right corner of the rectangle that bounds the ellipse.

Notes

The rectangle that bounds the ellipse determines the ellipse's shape and size. If, for example, you bound the ellipse with a square, _Ellipse draws a circle.

Upon completion of the _Ellipse procedure, your program can call the GrStatus function to determine the success of _Ellipse.

Status	Meaning
_GrClipped	Ellipse clipped to fit viewport
_GrInsufficientMemory	Not enough memory to complete operation
_GrInvalidParameter	Invalid argument in call to _Ellipse
_GrNoOutput	No ellipse drawn
_GrNotInProperMode	Invalid video display mode

Example

```
PROGRAM Ellipse;

USES
  MSGraph,   { contains graphics routines }
  Crt;       { contains the KeyPressed function }

VAR
  status: Integer;  { status of function call }

BEGIN
  { set the video mode to 320 by 200 graphics }
  status := _SetVideoMode(_MRes4Color);

  { draw an ellipse (border only) }
  _Ellipse(_GBorder, 55, 20, 130, 150);

  { draw a filled circle }
  _Ellipse(_GFillInterior, 180, 50, 280, 150);

  _SetTextPosition(23, 8);
  _OutText('Press any key to continue');

  WHILE (NOT KeyPressed) DO
    ;

  { restore the original video mode }
  status := _SetVideoMode(_DefaultMode);
END.
```

Related routines: _Arc, _Ellipse_w, _Ellipse_wxy, _FloodFill, _GrStatus, _SetColor, _SetFillMask

_Ellipse_w   MSGraph

Draws an ellipse using window coordinates.

Syntax
PROCEDURE _Ellipse_w(*fillControl*: Integer; *upperLeftx*, *upperLefty*, *lowerRightx*, *lowerRighty*: Double);

Arguments

fillControl specifies whether _Ellipse_w draws a filled ellipse or an ellipse border. The MSGraph unit defines two constants for fill control.

Constant	Meaning
_GFillInterior	Fill the ellipse
_GBorder	Draw the ellipse border only

upperLeftx and *upperLefty* are the window (floating-point) coordinates of the upper left corner of the rectangle that bounds the ellipse.

lowerRightx and *lowerRighty* are the window (floating-point) coordinates of the lower right corner of the rectangle that bounds the ellipse.

Notes

The _Ellipse_w function behaves identically to _Ellipse with the exception that it uses window coordinates.

Example

```
PROGRAM WindowShapes;

USES
  MSGraph,  { contains graphics routines }
  Crt;      { contains KeyPressed and ReadKey }

VAR
  status: Integer;
  upperLeft: _WXYCoord;
  lowerRight: _WXYCoord;
  startVect: _WXYCoord;
  stopVect: _WXYCoord;
  buffer: Char;

BEGIN
  { set the video mode to 320 by 200 graphics }
  status := _SetVideoMode(_MRes4Color);

  { define the window coordinates }
  _SetWindow(False, -1000.0, -1000.0,
    1000.0, 1000.0);
```

```pascal
  { draw a filled rectangle }
  _Rectangle_w(_GFillInterior, -800.0, -800.0,
    -400.0, 500.0);

  { draw an empty ellipse }
  _Ellipse_w(_GBorder, -300.0, -200.0,
    200.0, 300.0);

  { draw a pie shape }
  upperLeft.wx := 200.0;   upperLeft.wy := 300.0;
  lowerRight.wx := 600.0;  lowerRight.wy := 700.0;
  startVect.wx := 500.0;   startVect.wy := -300.0;
  stopVect.wx := 100.0;    stopVect.wy := 800.0;

  _Pie_wxy(_GBorder, upperLeft, lowerRight,
    startVect, stopVect);

  { draw a filled ellipse using _WXYCoord }
  upperLeft.wx := 500.0;   upperLeft.wy := -300.0;
  lowerRight.wx := 900.0;  lowerRight.wy := 0.0;

  _Ellipse_wxy(_GFillInterior,
    upperLeft, lowerRight);
  _SetTextPosition(23, 8);
  _OutText('Press any key to continue');

  { get a key from the user }
  buffer := ReadKey;

  { fill in the pie shape }
  _FloodFill_w(300.0, 400.0, _GetColor);

  WHILE (NOT KeyPressed) DO
    ;

  { restore the original video mode }
  status := _SetVideoMode(_DefaultMode);
END.
```

Related routines: _Arc, _Ellipse, _Ellipse_wxy, _FloodFill, _GrStatus, _SetColor, _SetFillMask

_Ellipse_wxy

MSGraph

Draws an ellipse using window coordinates.

Syntax
PROCEDURE _Ellipse_wxy(*fillControl*: Integer;
  VAR *upperLeft, lowerRight*: _WXYCoord);

Arguments
fillControl specifies whether _Ellipse_w draws a filled ellipse or an ellipse border. The MSGraph unit defines two constants for fill control.

Constant	Meaning
GFillInterior	Fill the ellipse
_GBorder	Draw the ellipse border only

upperLeft is a record of type _WXYCoord that contains the coordinates of the upper left corner of the rectangle that bounds the ellipse.

lowerRight is a record of type _WXYCoord that contains the coordinates of the lower right corner of the rectangle that bounds the ellipse.

Notes
The MSGraph unit defines the record type _WXYCoord as follows:

```
_WXYCoord = RECORD
  wx: Double;   { window x coordinate }
  wy: Double;   { window y coordinate }
END;
```

With the exception of using variables of type _WXYCoord, _Ellipse_wxy behaves exactly as _Ellipse_w does.

Example
See _Ellipse_w.

Related routines: _Arc, _Ellipse, _Ellipse_w, _FloodFill, _GrStatus, _SetColor, _SetFillMask

EnvCount
Dos

Returns the number of entries in the DOS environment.

Syntax
FUNCTION EnvCount: Word;

Arguments
None.

Notes
The DOS SET command creates environment entries.

Example
```
PROGRAM DisplayEnvironment;

USES
  Dos;

VAR
  index: Byte;        { environment index }
  numEntries: Byte;   { number of entries }

BEGIN
  { determine number of environment entries }
  numEntries := EnvCount;

  { display environment entries }
  FOR index := 1 TO numEntries DO
    Writeln(EnvStr(index));
END.
```

Related routines: EnvStr, GetEnv

EnvStr
Dos

Returns a DOS environment entry.

Syntax

FUNCTION EnvStr(*entryIndex*: <*integer type*>): STRING;

Arguments

entryIndex is the number of an environment entry. The first entry is numbered 1.

Notes

EnvStr returns a character string containing the entry name, the equal sign, and the entry value, such as PATH=C:\DOS.

Example

See EnvCount.

Related routines: EnvCount, GetEnv

Eof
System

Returns a file's end-of-file status.

Syntax

FUNCTION Eof[(VAR *filePointer*: <*file type*>)]: Boolean;

Arguments

filePointer is a file pointer to a typed, untyped, or text file.

Notes

Eof returns true if the file pointer is beyond the last element of a file. If the last element has not yet been encountered, Eof returns false.

Example

See Append.

Related routines: Append, Assign, Eoln, IOResult, Reset, Rewrite, Seek, SeekEof, SeekEoln

Eoln

System

Returns the end-of-line status for a text file.

Syntax
FUNCTION Eoln[(VAR *filePointer*: Text)]: Boolean;

Arguments
filePointer is a file pointer to an open text file. If you do not specify a file pointer, Eoln uses standard input.

Notes
The Eoln function recognizes the ASCII carriage-return character (ASCII 13) as the end-of-line character.

Example
```
PROGRAM EolnTest;

VAR
  letter: Char;  { letter read from keyboard }

BEGIN
  REPEAT
    Read(letter);
    Write(UpCase(letter));
  UNTIL (Eoln);
END.
```

Related routines: Eof, SeekEoln

Erase

System

Removes a file from disk.

Syntax
PROCEDURE Erase(VAR *filePointer*: <file type>);

Arguments

filePointer is a file pointer Assign associates with a file.

Notes

If the specified file does not exist, an I/O error occurs.

Erase works as the DOS DEL command does. After you erase a file, its contents are lost.

Example

```
PROGRAM MyErase;

VAR
  delFile: FILE;        { file to delete }
  sourceFile: STRING;   { filename to copy }

BEGIN
  { get sourcefile name }
  IF (ParamCount > 0) THEN
    sourceFile := ParamStr(1)
  ELSE
    BEGIN
      { get the filename from the user }
      Write('Enter source file: ');
      Readln(sourceFile);
    END;

  { assign the input filename to the file pointer }
  Assign(delFile, sourceFile);

  { erase the file }
  {$I-} { disable I/O checking }
  Erase(delFile);
  {$I+} { enable I/O checking }

  IF (IOResult <> 0) THEN  { test Erase's success }
    Writeln('Error erasing ', sourceFile)
  ELSE
    Writeln(sourceFile, ' deleted');
END.
```

Related routines: Rename, RmDir

Exec
Dos

Loads and executes a child process, temporarily suspending the parent process.

Syntax
PROCEDURE Exec(*commandName*: PathStr;
   commandLine: ComStr);

Arguments
commandName is a complete DOS pathname to the program that Exec is to execute as a child process.

commandLine is a string containing the command line arguments for the child process.

Notes
Exec does not allocate memory for the child process. Your program might need to set minimum stack and heap sizes using the {$M} compiler directive.

A child process can change interrupt handlers. Many programs that change interrupt handlers call SwapVectors before and after the call to Exec.

To execute a DOS internal command, your program must pass COMMAND.COM as the program name and the internal command as a command line argument as shown in the following example:

```
Exec('COMMAND.COM', '/C DIR');
```

The /C directs DOS to load a secondary command processor into memory only long enough to execute the DIR command.

When Exec completes execution, it assigns an error status value to the DosError global variable.

DosError	Meaning
2	File not found
8	Insufficient memory
10	Invalid environment
11	Invalid format

Example
See DosExitCode.

Related routines: DosExitCode, Exit, Halt, Keep, SwapVectors

Exit
System

Terminates the current procedure, function, or program.

Syntax
PROCEDURE Exit;

Arguments
None.

Notes
Within a function or procedure, calling Exit returns control to the calling routine.

Within the main program, calling Exit ends the program with an exit status of 0.

Example
```
PROGRAM ExitTest;

PROCEDURE ExitEarly;
BEGIN
  Writeln('About to exit procedure');
  Exit;
  Writeln('This line never executes');
END;

BEGIN
  ExitEarly;
  Writeln('About to exit program');
  Exit;
  Writeln('This line never executes');
END.
```

Related routines: DosExitCode, Exec, Halt, Keep

Exp

System

Returns the exponential of a real value.

Syntax
FUNCTION Exp(*value*: <*real type*>): <*real type*>;

Arguments
value is a floating-point number for which Exp returns the exponential.

Notes
The exponential of a number is the mathematical constant *e* raised to the number.

Example
```
PROGRAM ShowPower;

FUNCTION Power(value, exponent: Real): Real;
BEGIN
  Power := Exp(exponent * Ln(value));
END;

BEGIN
  Writeln('5 raised to the 2 is ',
    Power(5, 2):7:3);
  Writeln('2 raised to the 5.2 is ',
    Power(2, 5.2):7:3);
  Writeln('2 raised to the 16 is ',
    Power(2, 16):7:0);
END.
```

Related routine: Ln

FExpand

Dos

Builds a complete pathname.

Syntax

FUNCTION FExpand(*pathname*: PathStr): PathStr;

Arguments

pathname is a character string containing the initial pathname.

Notes

FExpand builds a complete DOS pathname by including a disk-drive letter and a root-relative subdirectory name.

If your initial path contains only an empty string, FExpand adds the current disk-drive letter and subdirectory name.

If the initial path contains a drive letter, FExpand uses the drive letter and adds only the subdirectory name.

If the initial path contains a subdirectory name, FExpand converts the subdirectory name to uppercase and changes the shorthand notations '.' or '..' to the corresponding directory names.

Example

```
PROGRAM ExpandIt;

USES
  Dos;  { contains FExpand function }

BEGIN
  Writeln(FExpand(''));
  Writeln(FExpand('FILENAME.EXT'));
END.
```

Related routines: FindFirst, FindNext, FSearch, FSplit, GetDir

FilePos   System

Returns the current position in a typed or untyped file.

Syntax

FUNCTION FilePos(VAR *filePointer*: <typed or untyped file>): LongInt;

Arguments

filePointer is a file pointer to an open non-text file.

Notes

FilePos does not work with text files.

FilePos returns the current position in the file. The first file entry is 0. If the current position is the end of the file, FilePos returns the same value that the FileSize function returns.

Example

```
PROGRAM FilePosition;

VAR
  data: FILE OF Integer;
  count: Integer;  { loop variable }

BEGIN
  Assign(data, 'DATA.TST');
  {$I-} { disable I/O checking }
  Rewrite(data);
  {$I+} { enable I/O checking }

  IF (IOResult <> 0) THEN
    Writeln('Error opening DATA.TST')
  ELSE
    BEGIN
      FOR count := 1 TO 100 DO
        Write(data, count);
      Seek(data, 0);
      Read(data, count);
      Writeln('Value at record 0 is ', count);
      Seek(data, 50);
      Read(data, count);
      Writeln('Value at record 50 is ', count);
      Writeln('Current record position is ',
        FilePos(data));
      Writeln('Current file size is ',
        FileSize(data));
      Close(data);
    END;
END.
```

Related routines: Eof, FileSize, Seek

FileSize
System

Returns the number of records in a non-text file.

Syntax
FUNCTION FileSize(VAR *filePointer*: <*typed or untyped file*>): LongInt;

Arguments
filePointer is a file pointer to an open non-text file.

Notes
FileSize does not work with text files.

For a typed file, FileSize returns the number of records in the file. For an untyped file, FileSize returns the number of blocks. The default block size is 128 bytes.

Example
See FilePos.

Related routines: BlockRead, BlockWrite, Eof, FilePos, Seek

FillChar
System

Fills a memory buffer with a byte or character value.

Syntax
PROCEDURE FillChar(VAR *buffer*: <*any type*>; *numBytes*: Word; *fillValue*: <*ordinal type*>);

Arguments
buffer is the memory buffer to which FillChar assigns the values.

numBytes specifies the number of bytes to assign to the memory buffer.

fillValue is the value written to the memory buffer.

Notes
FillChar does not provide range checking. Use the SizeOf function to prevent writing beyond the boundaries of the buffer.

Example
```
PROGRAM CharacterFilling;

VAR
  a: STRING;
  b: STRING;

BEGIN
  FillChar(a, 50, 'A');
  Writeln(a);
  FillChar(b, 30, 'B');
  Writeln(b);
END.
```

Related routines: Move, SizeOf

FindFirst — Dos

Searches a directory for the first file matching a given file specification.

Syntax
PROCEDURE FindFirst(*pattern*: PathStr; *attribute*: Word; VAR *fileInfo*: SearchRec);

Arguments
pattern is a character string containing the file specification to search for. If the pattern contains DOS wildcard characters, FindFirst expands the wildcard characters and returns the first matching file.

attribute specifies the file attribute of the target files. The DOS unit defines the following attribute constants.

Attribute	Value
ReadOnly	$01
Hidden	$02
SysFile	$04
VolumeID	$08
Directory	$10
Archive	$20

fileInfo is a record variable of type SearchRec that contains the file information for the first matching file.

```
SearchRec = RECORD
  Fill: ARRAY[1..21] OF Byte;  { reserved by DOS }
  Attr: Byte;                  { file attributes }
  Time: LongInt;               { last modification }
  Size: LongInt;               { file size in bytes }
  Name: STRING[12];            { name.ext }
END;
```

Notes

To search for a file using two or more attributes, simply join the attributes together using plus signs as follows:

```
attribute := Archive + ReadOnly;
```

When FindFirst completes execution, your program can test the global variable DosError to determine whether FindFirst was successful.

DosError

Value	Meaning
0	Successful
2	File not found
18	No matching files

FindFirst locates the first matching file, and FindNext locates subsequent files. Using the two procedures, your program can perform wildcard directory searches.

Example

```
PROGRAM DisplayDirectory;

USES
  Dos;
```

```
VAR
  fileInfo: SearchRec;

BEGIN
  { list files in the current directory }
  FindFirst('*.*', 0 { normal attribute },
    fileInfo);

  WHILE (DosError <> 18) DO
    BEGIN
      Writeln(fileInfo.Name);   { display filename }
      FindNext(fileInfo);       { get next file }
    END;
END.
```

Related routines: FindNext, UnpackTime

FindNext

Dos

Continues a directory search begun by the FindFirst procedure.

Syntax
PROCEDURE FindNext(VAR *fileInfo*: SearchRec);

Arguments
fileInfo is a record variable of type SearchRec that contains file information for the matching file.

```
SearchRec = RECORD
  Fill: ARRAY [1..21]OF Byte;  { reserved by DOS }
  Attr: Byte;                  { file attributes }
  Time: LongInt;               { last modification }
  Size: LongInt;               { file size in bytes }
  Name: STRING[12];            { name.ext }
END;
```

Notes
The FindFirst procedure identifies the search pattern and returns the first matching file. The FindNext procedure returns subsequent matching files.

When FindNext completes execution, your program can test the global variable DosError to determine whether FindNext was successful.

DosError Value	**Meaning**
0	Successful
18	No more files

Example
See FindFirst.

Related routines: FindFirst, UnpackTime

First
System

Returns the first value in a list of ordinal values.

Syntax
FUNCTION First(*ordinalType*): <*same type as argument*>;

Argument
ordinalType is any ordinal type name such as Integer, Boolean, and so on.

Notes
An ordinal type is a subrange type, predefined type, or program-defined enumerated type.

Example
```
PROGRAM PredSucc;

TYPE
  Months = (January, February, March, April,
    May, June, July, August, September, October,
    November, December);
```

```
Procedure DisplayMonthName(Month: Months);
BEGIN
  CASE Month OF
    January:   Writeln('January');
    February:  Writeln('February');
    March:     Writeln('March');
    April:     Writeln('April');
    May:       Writeln('May');
    June:      Writeln('June');
    July:      Writeln('July');
    August:    Writeln('August');
    September: Writeln('September');
    October:   Writeln('October');
    November:  Writeln('November');
    December:  Writeln('December');
  END;
END;

VAR
  month: Months;

BEGIN
  month := Succ(January);
  Write('The month after January is ');
  DisplayMonthName(month);
  month := Pred(December);
  Write('The month before December is ');
  DisplayMonthName(month);
  Write('The first month is ');
  DisplayMonthName(First(month));
  Write('The last month is ');
  DisplayMonthName(Last(month));
END.
```

Related routines: Dec, Inc, Last, Ord, Pred, Succ

_FloodFill   MSGraph

Fills a screen region with the current graphics fill pattern and color.

Syntax

PROCEDURE _FloodFill(x, y, borderColor: Integer);

Arguments

x and y are viewport coordinates within the region to be filled.

borderColor is the color of the line that borders the region to be filled.

Notes

If the x and y coordinates fall outside the graphics image, _FloodFill surrounds the image with color.

If the border line has any gaps, color will "leak" through the gaps.

When _FloodFill completes execution, your program can call _GrStatus to determine _FloodFill's success.

Status	Meaning
_GrClipped	Image clipped to fit viewport
_GrInsufficientMemory	Not enough memory to complete operation
_GrInvalidParameter	Invalid argument in call to _FloodFill
_GrNoOutput	No image drawn
_GrNotInProperMode	Invalid video display mode

Example

```
PROGRAM FillRectangle;

USES
  MSGraph,       { contains graphics functions }
  Crt;           { contains ReadKey function }

VAR
  status: Integer; { function return status }
  buffer: Char;    { buffer for ReadKey }

BEGIN
  status := _SetVideoMode(_MRes4Color);
```

```
_Rectangle(_GBorder, 50, 50, 200, 150);
_SetTextPosition(22, 8);
_OutText('Press any key to continue');

buffer := ReadKey;
_FloodFill(100, 100, _GetColor);
buffer := ReadKey;

status := _SetVideoMode(_DefaultMode);
END.
```

Related routines: _FloodFill_w, _GetColor, _GetFillMask, _SetColor, _SetFillMask

_FloodFill_w   MSGraph

Fills a screen region based upon window coordinates with the current graphics fill pattern and color.

Syntax
PROCEDURE _FloodFill_w(*realx, realy*: Double; *borderColor*: Integer);

Arguments
realx and *realy* are the *x* and *y* window (floating-point) coordinates of a location inside the region to be filled.

borderColor is the color of the line that borders the region to be filled.

Notes
With the exception that it uses window coordinates, _FloodFill_w works identically to _FloodFill.

Example
See _Ellipse_w.

Related routines: _FloodFill, _GetColor, _GetFillMask, _SetColor, _SetFillMask, _SetWindow

Flush
System

Writes the contents of a file buffer in memory to a text file.

Syntax
PROCEDURE Flush(*filePointer*: Text);

Arguments
filePointer is a file pointer to an open text file.

Notes
For better performance, many file operations are buffered in memory until a sector of information is ready for output. The Flush procedure forces the file buffer contents to be written to disk.

The QuickPascal Close procedure also flushes a file buffer to disk.

Related routines: Close, SetTextBuf

Frac
System

Returns the fractional part of a floating-point number.

Syntax
FUNCTION Frac(*value*: <*real type*>): <*real type*>;

Arguments
value is the floating-point value for which Frac returns the fractional portion.

Notes
The fractional portion of a floating-point value consists of the digits to the right of the decimal point.

Example

```
PROGRAM FractionalPart;

BEGIN
  Writeln(Frac(0.12345):8:5);
  Writeln(Frac(1.12345):8:5);
  Writeln(Frac(99.12345):8:5);
END.
```

Related routines: Int, Round, Trunc

FreeMem
System

Releases memory previously allocated by GetMem.

Syntax
PROCEDURE FreeMem(VAR *ptrVar*: Pointer;
   numBytes: Word);

Arguments
ptrVar is a pointer to the allocated memory FreeMem is to release.

numBytes is the number of bytes to release.

Notes
Do not intermix calls to GetMem and FreeMem with calls to New and Dispose. Doing so makes your program difficult to understand.

By default, if the pointer your program passes to FreeMem does not point to the heap, a heap error occurs.

Example

```
PROGRAM GetBigArray;

TYPE
  BigArray = ARRAY[1..2000] OF Integer;
```

(continued)

continued

```
VAR
  arrayPtr: ^BigArray;  { pointer to an array }
  index: Integer;       { array index }

BEGIN
  IF (MaxAvail < SizeOf(BigArray)) THEN
    Writeln('Insufficient heap space available')
  ELSE
    BEGIN
      { allocate memory for the array }
      GetMem(arrayPtr, SizeOf(BigArray));
      FOR index := 1 TO 2000 DO
        arrayPtr^[index] := index;

      FOR index := 1 TO 2000 DO
        Writeln(arrayPtr^[index]);

      FreeMem(arrayPtr, SizeOf(BigArray));
    END;
END.
```

Related routines: Addr, Dispose, GetMem, Mark, MaxAvail, MemAvail, New, Release, SizeOf

FSearch

Dos

Returns the directory location of the specified file.

Syntax
FUNCTION FSearch(*fileName*: PathStr;
  searchDirectories: <string type>): PathStr;

Arguments
fileName is the name of the file to search for.

searchDirectories is a list of pathnames, separated by semicolons, that FSearch will examine in searching for the file.

Notes

FSearch first looks for the file in the current directory and then walks through the list of search directories. The search continues until the file is found or the list of search directories is exhausted.

If FSearch locates the file in the current directory, it returns only the filename. If FSearch locates the file in one of the search-list directories, it returns a complete pathname. If FSearch does not find the file, it returns an empty string.

Example

```
PROGRAM FindFile;

USES
  Dos;

VAR
  location: PathStr;

BEGIN
  location := FSearch('QP.EXE',
    'C:\DOS;C:\;C:\QP');
  IF (location = '') THEN
    Writeln('File not found')
  ELSE
    Writeln('File located in ', location);
END.
```

Related routines: FExpand, FSplit

FSplit   Dos

Separates a complete DOS pathname into a drive, a directory, a filename, and an extension.

Syntax

PROCEDURE FSplit(*pathname*: PathStr; VAR *dir*: DirStr; VAR *filename*: NameStr; VAR *extension*: ExtStr);

Arguments

pathname is the complete pathname that FSplit separates into its elements.

dir is the file's DOS subdirectory path and disk drive.

filename is the file's eight-character name.

extension is the file's three-character extension.

Notes

If the pathname does not contain one of the component parts, such as a subdirectory path, FSplit assigns an empty string to the corresponding variable.

Example

```
PROGRAM SplitIt;

USES
  Dos;            { contains FSplit procedure }

VAR
  dir: DirStr;           { directory path }
  filename: NameStr;     { filename }
  extension: ExtStr;     { extension }

BEGIN
  FSplit('C:\QP\QP.EXE', dir, filename, extension);
  Writeln('Directory: ', dir);
  Writeln('Filename:  ', filename);
  Writeln('Extension: ', extension);
END.
```

Related routines: FExpand, FSearch

_GetActivePage   MSGraph

Returns the current active video-display page number.

Syntax

FUNCTION _GetActivePage: Integer;

Arguments
None.

Notes
The active video page is the page to which the _Outtext function writes text or to which the graphics functions draw images. The visual page is the page that appears on your screen. If you write output to an active page and then select that page as the visual page, the output will appear instantly on your screen.

The _GetVideoConfig procedure returns the number of available display pages for each mode.

Related routines: _GetVideoConfig, _GetVisualPage, _SetActivePage, _SetVisualPage

_GetArcInfo   MSGraph

Returns the viewport coordinates of the most recently drawn pie shape or arc.

Syntax
FUNCTION _GetArcInfo(VAR *startVector*, *stopVector*, *fillPoint*: _XYCoord): Boolean;

Arguments
startVector contains the *x* and *y* coordinates of the arc's start vector.

stopVector contains the *x* and *y* coordinates of the arc's stop vector.

fillPoint contains the *x* and *y* coordinates of a point within a pie shape that your program can pass to _FloodFill for filling.

Notes
_GetArcInfo returns true if an arc or pie shape has been drawn since the last time the screen was cleared or the

video mode was changed. If an arc or pie shape has not been drawn, _GetArcInfo returns false.

The MSGraph unit defines the record _XYCoord as follows:

```
_XYCoord = RECORD
  xcoord: Integer;
  ycoord: Integer;
END;
```

When _GetArcInfo completes execution, your program can call _GrStatus to determine additional error information.

Status	Meaning
_GrError	General graphics error
_GrNotInProperMode	Invalid video display mode

Example

```
PROGRAM GetArcInfo;

USES
  MSGraph,   { contains graphics routines }
  Crt;       { contains ReadKey function }

VAR
  status: Integer;
  start, stop, fillPt: _XYCoord;
  buffer: Char;
  arcDrawn: Boolean;

BEGIN
  { set the video mode to 320 by 200 graphics }
  status := _SetVideoMode(_MRes4Color);

  _SetTextPosition(23, 8);
  _OutText('Press any key to continue');

  _Pie(_GBorder,
    55, 20, 130, 150, 50, 150, 160, 80);

  buffer := ReadKey;

  arcDrawn := _GetArcInfo(start, stop, fillPt);
  _FloodFill(fillPt.xcoord, fillPt.ycoord,
    _GetColor);
```

```
  buffer := ReadKey;

  { restore the original video mode }
  status := _SetVideoMode(_DefaultMode);
END.
```

Related routines: _Arc, _FloodFill, _GrStatus, _Pie

_GetBkColor — MSGraph

Returns the current background color.

Syntax
FUNCTION _GetBkColor: LongInt;

Arguments
None.

Notes
In text mode, _GetBkColor returns a color index that corresponds to the following colors:

Color Index	Color	Color Index	Color
0	Black	8	Dark gray
1	Blue	9	Light blue
2	Green	10	Light green
3	Cyan	11	Light cyan
4	Red	12	Light red
5	Magenta	13	Light magenta
6	Brown	14	Yellow
7	White	15	Bright white

In graphics modes, _GetBkColor returns a value that corresponds to the VGA color constants defined in the MSGraph unit such as _Red, _Green, or _Blue.

Related routines: _RemapPalette, _SetBkColor

GetCBreak — Dos

Returns the current Ctrl+Break status.

Syntax
PROCEDURE GetCBreak(VAR *status*: Boolean);

Arguments
status is a Boolean value. If *status* is true, DOS checks for a user-entered Ctrl+Break after each system call. If false, DOS checks for Ctrl+Break only after console, printer, or serial port I/O.

Notes
The QuickPascal SetCBreak routine sets the Ctrl+Break status.

Example
```
PROGRAM GetStates;

USES
  Dos;

VAR
  ctrlBreak: Boolean;
  verify: Boolean;

BEGIN
  GetCBreak(ctrlBreak);
  Write('Extended Ctrl+Break checking ');
  IF (ctrlBreak) THEN
    Writeln('enabled')
  ELSE
    Writeln('disabled');

  GetVerify(verify);
  Write('Disk verification ');
  IF (verify) THEN
    Writeln('enabled')
  ELSE
    Writeln('disabled');
```

```
    Writeln('Extended Ctrl+Break checking and disk');
    Writeln('verification produce unnecessary');
    Writeln('program overhead.');
END.
```

Related routines: GetVerify, SetCBreak, SetVerify

_GetColor   MSGraph

Returns the current color index.

Syntax
FUNCTION _GetColor: Integer;

Arguments
None.

Notes
The _GetColor function returns the current palette color index.

Example
```
PROGRAM FillRectangle;

USES
  MSGraph,        { contains graphics functions }
  Crt;            { contains ReadKey function }

VAR
  status: Integer;  { function return status }
  buffer: Char;     { buffer for ReadKey }

BEGIN
  status := _SetVideoMode(_MRes4Color);

  _Rectangle(_GBorder, 50, 50, 200, 150);
  _SetTextPosition(22, 8);
  _OutText('Press any key to continue');
```

(continued)

continued

```
  buffer := ReadKey;
  _FloodFill(100, 100, _GetColor);
  buffer := ReadKey;

  status := _SetVideoMode(_DefaultMode);
END.
```

Related routines: _GetTextColor, _SetColor

_GetCurrentPosition — MSGraph

Returns the current graphics position.

Syntax
PROCEDURE _GetCurrentPosition(VAR *xyPos*: _XYCoord);

Arguments
xyPos is a variable of type _XYCoord that contains the viewport coordinates of the current position.

```
_XYCoord = RECORD
  xcoord: Integer;
  ycoord: Integer;
END;
```

Notes
The current graphics position is the location of the last _LineTo, _MoveTo, or _OutGText operation. By default, the current graphics position is the center of the viewport.

Font-based output occurs at the current graphics position. Text output occurs at the current text position.

When _GetCurrentPosition completes execution, your program can test its success by calling _GrStatus.

Status	Meaning
_GrNotInProperMode	Invalid video display mode

Related routines: _GetCurrentPosition_wxy, _GetTextPosition, _GrStatus, _LineTo, _MoveTo

_GetCurrentPosition_wxy   MSGraph

Returns the current graphics position, using window coordinates.

Syntax
PROCEDURE _GetCurrentPosition_wxy(VAR *realxy*: _WXYCoord);

Arguments
realxy is a record of type _WXYCoord that contains the window (floating-point) coordinates of the current position.

```
_WXYCoord = RECORD
  wx: Double;   { window x coordinate }
  wy: Double;   { window y coordinate }
END;
```

Notes
With the exception that it uses the _WXYCoord record type, _GetCurrentPosition_wxy behaves exactly as _GetCurrentPosition does.

Related routines: _GetCurrentPosition, _GetTextPosition, _GrStatus, _LineTo, _MoveTo

GetDate   Dos

Returns the current system date.

Syntax
PROCEDURE GetDate(VAR *year, month, day, weekday*: Word);

Arguments
year is the current year (from 1980 through 2009).

month is the current month (from 1 through 12).

day is the current day of the month (from 1 through 31).

weekday is the day of the week (from 0 through 6; 0 is Sunday, 6 is Saturday).

Notes
The GetDate procedure returns the DOS system date set by the DATE command.

Example
```
PROGRAM GetSystemDateTime;

USES
  Dos;  { contains GetDate and GetTime procedures }

VAR
  day, month, year, weekday: Integer;
  hour, minute, second, hund: Integer;

BEGIN
  GetDate(year, month, day, weekday);
  GetTime(hour, minute, second, hund);

  Writeln('Current date: ',
    month, '/', day, '/', year);
  Writeln('Current time: ',
    hour, ':', minute, ':', second, '.', hund);
END.
```

Related routines: GetTime, SetDate, SetTime

GetDir   System

Returns the current directory for the specified disk drive.

Syntax
PROCEDURE GetDir(*driveNumber*: Byte;
    VAR *directory*: <string type>);

Arguments
driveNumber is the desired drive number from 0 through 26. (0 is the current drive, A is 1, B is 2, C is 3, and so on.)

directory is a string variable to which GetDir assigns the current directory.

Notes
If the specified drive is not ready, GetDir returns the drive letter followed by a colon and a backslash to indicate the root directory.

If the drive is invalid, GetDir returns a meaningless character followed by a colon and a backslash.

Example
```
PROGRAM GetDirectory;

VAR
  directory: STRING;   { current directory }

BEGIN
  GetDir(0, directory);
  Writeln('The current directory is ', directory);
END.
```

Related routines: ChDir, MkDir, RmDir

GetEnv   Dos

Returns a DOS environment entry's setting.

Syntax
FUNCTION GetEnv(*entryName*: <*string type*>): <*string type*>;

Arguments
entryName is the name of an environment entry such as PATH.

Notes
Do not include the equal sign in the entry name.

The value that GetEnv returns does not include the environment entry name or the equal sign.

Example

```
PROGRAM ShowPath;

USES
  Dos;            { contains environment functions }

VAR
  path: STRING;   { current PATH entry }

BEGIN
  path := GetEnv('PATH');

  IF (path = '') THEN
    Writeln('PATH entry not defined')
  ELSE
    Writeln('PATH=', path);
END.
```

Related routines: EnvCount, EnvStr

GetFAttr

Dos

Returns a file's attributes.

Syntax
PROCEDURE GetFAttr(VAR *filePointer*: <*file type*>;
  VAR *attributes*: Word);

Arguments
filePointer is a file pointer assigned to a file. The file must not be open.

attributes is a variable of type Word to which GetFAttr assigns the file attributes.

Notes
The DOS unit defines the following file-attribute values:

Attribute	Value
ReadOnly	$01
Hidden	$02

Attribute	Value
SysFile	$04
VolumeID	$08
Directory	$10
Archive	$20

Upon completion, GetFAttr assigns its status value to the DosError global variable.

Status	Meaning
0	Successful
3	Path not found
5	Access denied

Related routines: Assign, FindFirst, FindNext, SetFAttr

_GetFillMask — MSGraph

Returns the current fill mask.

Syntax
FUNCTION _GetFillMask(VAR *mask*: _FillMask): Boolean;

Arguments
mask is an 8-by-8 array of bits in which each bit corresponds to a pixel in the fill mask. If the bit is 1, the pixel is on. If the bit is 0, the pixel is off.

Notes
The MSGraph unit defines the type _FillMask as follows:

```
_FillMask = ARRAY[0..7] OF Byte;
```

When _GetFillMask completes execution, it returns false if the program has not yet defined a fill mask and true if the program has defined a fill mask with _SetFillMask.

The _GrStatus function returns the following status values for _GetFillMask.

Status	Meaning
_GrError	General graphics error
_GrNotInProperMode	Invalid video display mode

Example

```
PROGRAM GetFillMask;

USES
  MSGraph,  { contains graphics routines }
  Crt;      { contains the KeyPressed function }

PROCEDURE FillBox;
CONST
  bigDots: _FillMask =
    (204, 204, 51, 51, 204, 204, 51, 51);
  defaultMask: _FillMask =
    (255, 255, 255, 255, 255, 255, 255, 255);

VAR
  maskDefined: Boolean;
  fillMask: _FillMask;

BEGIN
  { save the current fill mask }
  maskDefined := _GetFillMask(fillMask);

  _SetFillMask(bigDots);
  _Rectangle(_GFillInterior, 100, 50, 150, 150);

  { restore previous fill mask }
  IF (maskDefined) THEN
    _SetFillMask(fillMask)
  ELSE
    _SetFillMask(defaultMask);
END;

VAR
  status: Integer;  { status of function call }

BEGIN
  { set the video mode to 320 by 200 graphics }
  status := _SetVideoMode(_MRes4Color);

  FillBox;
```

```
{ draw a rectangle with the default mask }
_Rectangle(_GFillInterior, 200, 50, 250, 150);

_SetTextPosition(23, 8);
_OutText('Press any key to continue');

WHILE (NOT KeyPressed) DO
  ;

{ restore the original video mode }
status := _SetVideoMode(_DefaultMode);
END.
```

Related routines: _Ellipse, _FloodFill, _GetLineStyle, _Pie, _Rectangle, _SetFillMask, _SetLineStyle

_GetFontInfo   MSGraph

Returns the current graphics font characteristics.

Syntax
FUNCTION _GetFontInfo(VAR *fontInformation*:
  _FontInfo): Integer;

Arguments
fontInformation is a record of type _FontInfo that contains the following information:

```
_FontInfo = RECORD
  FontType : Integer;   { bit 0 set, vector;
                          else, raster }
  Ascent   : Integer;   { pixels from top to
                          baseline }
  PixWidth : Integer;   { width in pixels
                          (0 = proportional) }
  PixHeight: Integer;   { height in pixels }
  AvgWidth : Integer;   { average character width }
  FileName : CSTRING[80]; { font file including
                            path }
  FaceName : CSTRING[31]; { font name }
END;
```

Notes

If successful, _GetFontInfo returns the value 0; otherwise, it returns the value −1.

The _GrStatus function returns the following status value for _GetFontInfo:

Status	Meaning
_GrError	General graphics error

Related routines: _GetGTextExtent, _GrStatus, _OutGText, _RegisterFonts, _SetFont, _UnRegisterFonts

GetFTime
Dos

Returns the date and time stamp of the last file modification.

Syntax
PROCEDURE GetFTime(VAR *filePointer*: <file type>;
 VAR *timeStamp*: LongInt);

Arguments
filePointer is a file pointer to an open file.

timeStamp is a date and time stamp compressed into four bytes.

Notes
The UnpackTime procedure converts the date and time to a format your program can easily work with.

Upon completion, GetFTime assigns one of the following values to the global variable DosError:

Status	Meaning
0	Successful
6	Invalid file handle

Related routines: FindFirst, FindNext, PackTime, SetFTime, UnpackTime

_GetGTextExtent — MSGraph

Returns the pixel width of a text font.

Syntax
FUNCTION _GetGTextExtent(*textStr*: CSTRING):
  Integer;

Arguments
textStr is the character string _OutGtext is to display.

Notes
Use _GetGTextExtent to determine the size of text that uses proportionally spaced fonts.

The _GrStatus function returns the following status value for _GetGTextExtent:

Status	Meaning
_GrError	General graphics error

Example
See _SetFont.

Related routines: _GetFontInfo, _GrStatus, _OutGText, _RegisterFonts, _SetFont, _UnRegisterFonts

_GetGTextVector — MSGraph

Returns the orientation of text the _OutGText function is to display.

Syntax
PROCEDURE _GetGTextVector(VAR *x, y*: Integer);

Arguments
x and *y* specify the text vector as shown in the following table.

x	y	Orientation
1	0	Horizontal text
0	1	90-degree rotation
-1	0	180 degree rotation
0	-1	270-degree rotation

Notes

The _SetGTextVector function defines the text orientation. The text orientation affects _OutGText only.

Related routines: _OutGText, _SetGTextVector

_GetImage
MSGraph

Copies a graphics image from the screen to memory.

Syntax
PROCEDURE _GetImage(*upperLeftx*, *upperLefty*, *lowerRightx*, *lowerRighty*: Integer; VAR *imageBuffer*);

Arguments
upperLeftx and *upperLefty* are the x and y coordinates of the upper left corner of the rectangle that bounds the graphics image.

lowerRightx and *lowerRighty* are the x and y coordinates of the lower right corner of the rectangle that bounds the graphics image.

imageBuffer is the buffer that stores the image.

Notes
To copy an image from the screen, you must define a rectangle that encloses the image and then copy the rectangle's contents.

The _ImageSize function tells you how large your buffer should be.

The _GrStatus function returns the following error status values for _GetImage.

Status	Meaning
_GrError	General graphics error
_GrNotInProperMode	Invalid video display mode
_GrParameterAltered	Parameters altered to remain within range

Example

```
PROGRAM MoveComputer;

USES
  MSGraph,   { contains graphics routines }
  Crt;       { contains the KeyPressed function }

VAR
  status: Integer;      { status of function call }
  imageBuffer: ^Byte;   { pointer to image }
  bufSize: Word;        { image size in bytes }
  xPosition: Integer;   { image position }

BEGIN
  { set the video mode to 320 by 200 graphics }
  status := _SetVideoMode(_MRes4Color);

  { draw the computer chassis }
  _Rectangle(_GBorder, 100, 100, 190, 120);
  { draw the disk drives }
  _Rectangle(_GBorder, 150, 105, 165, 115);
  _Rectangle(_GBorder, 170, 105, 185, 115);

  { draw the monitor }
  _Rectangle(_GBorder, 120, 65, 170, 95);
  _Rectangle(_GFillInterior, 125, 70, 165, 90);

  { determine the image size }
  bufSize := _ImageSize(100, 65, 190, 120);

  { allocate memory for the image }
  GetMem(imageBuffer, bufSize);

  { capture the image }
  _GetImage(100, 65, 190, 120, imageBuffer^);

  FOR xPosition := 100 DOWNTO 20 DO
    BEGIN
```

(continued)

continued

```
     { erase the current image }
     _PutImage(xPosition, 65, imageBuffer^,
       _GXOR);
     { draw the image moved slightly to the left }
     _PutImage(xPosition - 1, 65, imageBuffer^,
       _GXOR);
   END;

  { release memory allocated for image buffer }
  FreeMem(imageBuffer, bufSize);

  _SetTextPosition(23, 8);
  _OutText('Press any key to continue');

  WHILE (NOT KeyPressed) DO
    ;

  { restore the original video mode }
  status := _SetVideoMode(_DefaultMode);
END.
```

Related routines: _GetImage_w, _GetImage_wxy, _ImageSize, _PutImage

_GetImage_w   MSGraph

Copies a graphics image from the screen to memory, using window coordinates.

Syntax
PROCEDURE _GetImage_w(*upperLeftx, upperLefty, lowerRightx, lowerRighty*: Double; VAR *imagebuffer*);

Arguments
upperLeftx and *upperLefty* contain the *x* and *y* window (floating-point) coordinates of the upper left corner of the rectangle that borders the image.

lowerRightx and *lowerRighty* contain the *x* and *y* window (floating-point) coordinates of the lower right corner of the rectangle that borders the image.

imageBuffer is the buffer that stores the image.

Notes
With the exception that _GetImage_w uses window coordinates, its processing is identical to that of _GetImage.

Example
See _GetImage.

Related routines: _GetImage, _GetImage_wxy, _ImageSize_w, _PutImage_w

_GetImage_wxy   MSGraph

Copies a graphics image from the screen to memory, using window coordinates.

Syntax
PROCEDURE _GetImage_wxy(VAR *upperLeft*,
   lowerRight: _WXYCoord; VAR *imageBuffer*);

Arguments
upperLeft is a record of type _WXYCoord that contains the window (floating-point) coordinates of the upper left corner of the rectangle that borders the image.

lowerRight is a record of type _WXYCoord that contains the window (floating-point) coordinates of the lower right corner of the rectangle that borders the image.

imageBuffer is the buffer that stores the image.

Notes
The MSGraph unit defines the record _WXYCoord as follows:

```
_WXYCoord = RECORD
  wx: Double;    { window x coordinate }
  wy: Double;    { window y coordinate }
END;
```

With the exception that _GetImage_wxy uses window coordinates, its processing is identical to that of _GetImage.

Example
See _GetImage.

Related routines: _GetImage, _GetImage_w, _ImageSize_wxy, _PutImage_w

GetIntVec   Dos

Returns the interrupt vector address for the specified interrupt.

Syntax
PROCEDURE GetIntVect(*interruptNumber*: Byte;
   VAR *vectorAddress*: Pointer);

Arguments
interruptNumber is a byte value (from 0 through 255) that specifies the desired interrupt.

vectorAddress is the 32-bit address of the interrupt handler.

Notes
Programs that change an interrupt handler must first save the current handler so that they can restore the handler before the program completes execution.

Related routine: SetIntVec

_GetLineStyle   MSGraph

Returns the current line-style mask that controls lines drawn by _LineTo and _Rectangle.

Syntax
FUNCTION _GetLineStyle: Word;

Arguments
None.

Notes
A line style is a 16-bit value that corresponds to 16 pixels in a line. If a bit in the line style is 1, the pixel is on. If a bit in the line style is 0, the corresponding pixel is off.

The default mask is $FFFF, or all bits set to 1, a solid line.

Related routines: _LineTo, _Pie, _Rectangle, _SetLineStyle

GetMem   MSGraph

Allocates the specified amount of memory from the heap.

Syntax
PROCEDURE GetMem(VAR *pointerVariable*:
  <*pointer type*>; *numBytes*: Word);

Arguments
pointerVariable is the variable to which GetMem assigns the address of the allocated memory.

numBytes specifies the number of bytes GetMem is to allocate from the heap.

Notes
Do not intermix calls to GetMem and FreeMem with calls to New and Dispose. Doing so will make your program difficult to understand.

GetMem cannot allocate a variable larger than 65,520 bytes.

If insufficient heap space is available, an error occurs. Use the MaxAvail and MemAvail functions to determine the amount of available heap space.

Example
See FreeMem.

Related routines: Dispose, FreeMem, Mark, MaxAvail, MemAvail, New, Release

_GetPhysCoord
MSGraph

Converts viewport coordinates to physical screen coordinates.

Syntax
PROCEDURE _GetPhysCoord(*viewportx*, *viewporty*: Integer; VAR *physxy*: _XYCoord);

Arguments
viewportx and *viewporty* are the viewport coordinates to be converted to physical coordinates.

physxy is a record of type _XYCoord that contains the physical *x* and *y* coordinates that correspond to the viewport coordinates.

Notes
The MSGraph unit defines the record type _XYCoord as follows:

```
_XYCoord = RECORD
  xcoord: Integer;
  ycoord: Integer;
END;
```

The _GrStatus function returns the following status value for _GetPhysCoord:

Status	Meaning
_GrNotInProperMode	Invalid video display mode

Related routines: _GetViewCoord, _GrStatus, _SetViewOrg, _SetViewport

_GetPixel
MSGraph

Returns the color of a pixel at the specified viewport coordinates.

Syntax
FUNCTION _GetPixel(x, y: Integer): Integer;

Arguments
x and y are the viewport coordinates of the desired pixel.

Notes
If successful, _GetPixel returns a color index; otherwise, _GetPixel returns −1.

The _GrStatus function returns the following status values for _GetPixel:

Status	Meaning
_GrError	General graphics error
_GrNotInProperMode	Invalid video display mode

Related routines: _GetPixel_w, _GrStatus, _SetColor, _SetPixel

_GetPixel_w
MSGraph

Returns the color of a pixel at the specified window coordinates.

Syntax
FUNCTION _GetPixel_w(realx, realy: Double): Integer;

Arguments
realx and *realy* are the x and y window (floating-point) coordinates of the desired pixel.

Notes

With the exception that it uses window coordinates, _GetPixel_w behaves identically to _GetPixel.

Related routines: _GetPixel, _GrStatus, _SetColor, _SetPixel_w

_GetTextColor   MSGraph

Returns the current text color used for output by _OutText and _OutMem.

Syntax
FUNCTION _GetTextColor: Integer;

Arguments
None.

Notes

The _SetTextColor function sets the color that is used by _OutText and _OutMem for text output. _OutGText uses the current graphics color set by _SetColor.

Related routines: _GetBkColor, _OutMem, _OutText, _SetBkColor, _SetTextColor

_GetTextCursor   MSGraph

Returns the text-mode cursor attributes.

Syntax
FUNCTION _GetTextCursor: Word;

Arguments
None.

Notes

The value returned by _GetTextCursor contains the current cursor size. The high-order byte contains the cursor's starting scan line; the low-order byte contains the cursor's ending scan line.

The _GrStatus function returns the following status value for _GetTextCursor:

Status	Meaning
_GrNotInProperMode	Invalid video display mode

Related routines: _GrStatus, _SetTextCursor

_GetTextPosition   MSGraph

Returns the current text row and column position.

Syntax
PROCEDURE _GetTextPosition(VAR *row*,
    column: Integer);

Arguments
row is the current text row from 1 through 25 (through 43 or 50 with an EGA or a VGA monitor).

column is the current text column from 1 through 80.

Notes
The current text position dictates where _OutText and _OutMem will display output. The current text position does not affect graphics output or font text displayed by _OutGText.

Related routines: _OutMem, _OutText, _SetTextPosition

_GetTextWindow — MSGraph

Returns the row and column positions of the current text window.

Syntax
PROCEDURE _GetTextWindow(VAR *topRow*, *leftColumn*, *bottomRow*, *rightColumn*: Integer);

Arguments
topRow and *leftColumn* specify the text window's upper left corner, or home position.

bottomRow and *rightColumn* specify the text window's lower right corner.

Notes
Text output by _OutText or _OutMem is restricted to the current text window. By default, the text window is the entire screen.

The current text window does not affect font output from _OutGText. Instead, font output is restricted to the current viewport.

Related routines: _SetTextPosition, _SetTextWindow, _WrapOn

GetTime — Dos

Gets the current system time.

Syntax
PROCEDURE GetTime(VAR *hours*, *minutes*, *seconds*, *hundredths*: Word);

Arguments

hours is the current hour from 0 through 23. 0 is midnight, and 12 is noon.

minutes is the current minute from 0 through 59.

seconds is the current second from 0 through 59.

hundredths is the current hundredth of a second from 0 through 99.

Notes

The GetTime procedure returns the system date set by the DOS TIME command.

Example

See GetDate.

Related routines: GetDate, SetDate, SetTime

GetVerify   Dos

Returns the current disk-verification state.

Syntax

PROCEDURE GetVerify(VAR *verifyState*: Boolean);

Arguments

verifyState is a Boolean variable that, when true, indicates that disk verification is enabled. When *verifyState* is false, disk verification is off.

Notes

The DOS VERIFY command enables and disables disk verification.

Example

See GetCBreak.

Related routines: GetCBreak, SetCBreak, SetVerify

_GetVideoConfig   MSGraph

Returns information about the current video display mode.

Syntax
PROCEDURE _GetVideoConfig(VAR *videoInfo*: _VideoConfig);

Arguments
videoInfo is a record variable of type _VideoConfig defined in the MSGraph unit as follows:

```
_VideoConfig = RECORD
  NumXPixels   : Integer;   { horiz. resolution }
  NumYPixels   : Integer;   { vertical resolution }
  NumTextCols  : Integer;   { text columns }
  NumTextRows  : Integer;   { text rows }
  NumColors    : Integer;   { number of colors }
  BitsPerPixel : Integer;   { bits per pixel }
  NumVideoPages: Integer;   { display pages }
  Mode         : Integer;   { current video mode }
  Adapter      : Integer;   { video adapter type }
  Monitor      : Integer;   { monitor type }
  Memory       : Integer;   { video memory }
END;
```

Notes
The Adapter field can contain the following values:

Adapter	Meaning
_MDPA	Monochrome display adapter
_CGA	Color graphics adapter
_EGA	Enhanced graphics adapter
_VGA	Video graphics array
_MCGA	Multicolor graphics array
_HGC	Hercules graphics card
_OCGA	Olivetti color graphics adapter
_OEGA	Olivetti enhanced graphics adapter
_OVGA	Olivetti video graphics array

The Monitor field can contain the following values:

Monitor	Meaning
_Mono	Monochrome
_Color	Color or enhanced color
_EnhColor	Enhanced color
_AnalogMono	Analog monochrome only
_AnalogColor	Analog color only
_Analog	Analog color or monochrome

Example

```
PROGRAM VideoConfiguration;

USES
  MSGraph;        { contains _GetVideoConfig }

VAR
  videoInfo: _VideoConfig;  { video configuration }

BEGIN
  _GetVideoConfig(videoInfo);

  Writeln('Number of X pixels: ',
    videoInfo.NumXPixels);
  Writeln('Number of Y pixels: ',
    videoInfo.NumYPixels);
  Writeln('Number of text columns: ',
    videoInfo.NumTextCols);
  Writeln('Number of text rows: ',
    videoInfo.NumTextRows);
  Writeln('Number of available colors: ',
    videoInfo.NumColors);
  Writeln('Bits per pixel: ',
    videoInfo.BitsPerPixel);
  Writeln('Number of video display pages: ',
    videoInfo.NumVideoPages);
  Write('Current video mode: ');

  { because we are not selecting a graphics mode
    and because Writeln works only in text mode,
    we will test only for text modes }
```

(continued)

continued

```
CASE (videoInfo.Mode) OF
  _TextBW40: Writeln('40-column BW');
  _TextC40:  Writeln('40-column color');
  _TextBW80: Writeln('80-column BW');
  _TextC80:  Writeln('80-column color');
END;

Write('Current video adapter type: ');

CASE (videoInfo.Adapter) OF
  _MDPA: Writeln('Monochrome');
  _CGA:  Writeln('Color graphics');
  _EGA:  Writeln('Enhanced graphics');
  _VGA:  Writeln('Video graphics array');
  _MCGA: Writeln('Multicolor graphics');
  _HGC:  Writeln('Hercules graphics');
  _OCGA: Writeln('Olivetti color graphics');
  _OEGA: Writeln('Olivetti enhanced graphics');
  _OVGA: Writeln('Olivetti vid. graphics array');
END;

Write('Current monitor type: ');

CASE (videoInfo.Monitor) OF
  _Mono:        Writeln('Monochrome');
  _Color:       Writeln('Color or enhanced');
  _EnhColor:    Writeln('Enhanced color');
  _AnalogMono:  Writeln('Analog monochrome');
  _AnalogColor: Writeln('Analog color');
  _Analog:      Writeln('Analog color or monochrome');
END;

Writeln('Video memory: ', videoInfo.Memory,
  ' KB');
END.
```

Related routines: _SetVideoMode, _SetVideoModeRows

_GetViewCoord   MSGraph

Converts physical coordinates to viewport coordinates.

Syntax

PROCEDURE _GetViewCoord(*physx*, *physy*: Integer;
  VAR *viewxy*: _XYCoord);

Arguments

physx and *physy* are the physical coordinates to be converted to viewport coordinates.

viewxy is a record of type _XYCoord that contains the viewport coordinates that correspond to the physical coordinates.

Notes

The MSGraph unit defines the record type _XYCoord as follows:

```
_XYCoord = RECORD
  xcoord: Integer;
  ycoord: Integer;
END;
```

Upon completion of the _GetViewCoord procedure, the _GrStatus function returns the following error status value:

Status	Meaning
_GrNotInProperMode	Invalid video display mode

Related routines: _GetPhysCoord, _GetViewCoord_w, _GetViewCoord_wxy, _GrStatus, _SetViewport

_GetViewCoord_w   MSGraph

Converts window coordinates to viewport coordinates.

Syntax

PROCEDURE _GetViewCoord_w(*realx*, *realy*: Double;
  VAR *viewxy*: _XYCoord);

Arguments

realx and *realy* are the window (floating-point) coordinates to be converted to viewport coordinates.

viewxy is a record of type _XYCoord that contains the viewport coordinates that correspond to the window coordinates.

Notes

The MSGraph unit defines the record type _XYCoord as follows:

```
_XYCoord = RECORD
  xcoord: Integer;
  ycoord: Integer;
END;
```

The _GrStatus function returns the following status value for _GetViewCoord_w:

Status	Meaning
_GrNotInProperMode	Invalid video display mode

Related routines: _GetViewCoord, _GetViewCoord_wxy, _GrStatus, _SetViewport, _SetWindow

_GetViewCoord_wxy   MSGraph

Converts window coordinates to viewport coordinates.

Syntax

PROCEDURE _GetViewCoord_wxy(VAR *realxy*: _WXYCoord; VAR *viewxy*: _XYCoord);

Arguments

realxy is a record of type _WXYCoord that contains the window (floating-point) coordinates to be converted to viewport coordinates.

viewxy is a record of type _XYCoord that contains the viewport coordinates that correspond to the window coordinates.

Notes

The MSGraph unit defines the record type _WXYCoord as follows:

```
_WXYCoord = RECORD
  wx: Double;    { window x coordinate }
  wy: Double;    { window y coordinate }
END;
```

The MSGraph unit defines the record type _XYCoord as follows:

```
_XYCoord = RECORD
  xcoord: Integer;
  ycoord: Integer;
END;
```

With the exception that it uses the _WXYCoord record type, _GetViewCoord_wxy behaves exactly as _GetViewCoord_w does.

Related routines: _GetViewCoord, _GetViewCoord_w, _GrStatus, _SetViewport, _SetWindow

_GetVisualPage   MSGraph

Returns the number of the current visual page.

Syntax
FUNCTION _GetVisualPage: Integer;

Arguments
None.

Notes
The visual page is the video display page that appears on the screen. The active page is the display page to which _OutText writes text or to which graphics images are drawn. If you write output to the active page and then select that page as the visual page, the output will appear on the screen instantly.

A program that changes video display pages should always save the current visual page at the outset and then restore it before ending.

The _GetVideoConfig function returns the number of available video display pages for the current display mode.

Related routines: _GetActivePage, _SetActivePage, _SetVisualPage

_GetWindowCoord   MSGraph

Converts viewport coordinates to window coordinates.

Syntax
PROCEDURE _GetWindowCoord(*viewx*, *viewy*: Integer; VAR *realxy*: _WXYCoord);

Arguments
viewx and *viewy* are the viewport coordinates to be converted to window coordinates.

realxy is a record of type _WXYCoord that contains the window (floating-point) coordinates that correspond to the viewport coordinates.

Notes
The MSGraph unit defines the record type _WXYCoord as follows:

```
_WXYCoord = RECORD
  wx: Double;    { window x coordinate }
  wy: Double;    { window y coordinate }
END;
```

The _GrStatus function returns the following status value for _GetWindowCoord:

Status	Meaning
_GrNotInProperMode	Invalid video display mode

Related routines: _GetPhysCoord, _GetViewCoord, _GetViewCoord_w, _GetViewCoord_wxy, _GrStatus, _SetWindow

_GetWriteMode — MSGraph

Returns the logical line mode used in conjunction with the current line style.

Syntax
FUNCTION _GetWriteMode: Integer;

Arguments
None.

Notes
The logical write mode determines how lines are drawn on your screen in cases in which pixels are currently on. The following line modes are supported:

Mode	Action
_GPSET	Causes the line to be drawn in the current color (default)
_GAND	Performs a logical AND of the pixels in each line position
_GOR	Performs a logical OR of the pixels in each line position
_GXOR	Performs an exclusive OR of the line pixels with the current screen pixels
_GPRESET	Draws the line inverting the current line style

The _GrStatus function returns the following status value for _GetWriteMode:

Status	Meaning
_GrNotInProperMode	Invalid video display mode

Related routines: _GrStatus, _LineTo, _PutImage, _Rectangle, _SetLineStyle, _SetWriteMode

GotoXY
Crt

Moves the cursor to the specified column and row position.

Syntax
PROCEDURE GotoXY(*column, row*: Byte);

Arguments
column is the desired screen column position along the *x* axis from 1 through 80.

row is the desired screen row position along the *y* axis from 1 through 25 (through 43 and 50 for EGA and VGA).

Notes
Be careful; notice the order of GotoXY's parameters. The column value comes first.

Example
See ClrEol.

Related routines: WhereX, WhereY, Window

_GrStatus
MSGraph

Returns the success status of the most recent graphics call.

Syntax
FUNCTION _GrStatus: Integer;

Arguments
None.

Notes
_GrStatus returns positive and negative values. Values less than zero are errors, and values greater than zero are warnings.

Constant	Status Value
_GrOk	0
_GrError	−1
_GrModeNotSupported	−2
_GrNotInProperMode	−3
_GrInvalidParameter	−4
_GrFontFileNotFound	−5
_GrInvalidFontFile	−6
_GrCorruptedFontFile	−7
_GrInsufficientMemory	−8
_GrInvalidImageBuffer	−9
_GrNoOutput	1
_GrClipped	2
_GrParameterAltered	3

Example

```
PROGRAM GrStatus;

USES
  MSGraph;  { contains graphics routines }

BEGIN
  _Rectangle(_GFillInterior, 100, 50, 200, 150);

  CASE (_GrStatus) OF
    _GrOk: Writeln('_GrOk');
    _GrError: Writeln('_GrError');
    _GrModeNotSupported:
      Writeln('_GrModeNotSupported');
    _GrNotInProperMode:
      Writeln('_GrNotInProperMode');
    _GrInvalidParameter:
      Writeln('_GrInvalidParameter');
    _GrInsufficientMemory:
      Writeln('_GrInsufficientMemory');
    _GrNoOutput: Writeln('_GrNoOutput');
    _GrClipped: Writeln('_GrClipped');
    _GrParameterAltered:
      Writeln('_GrParameterAltered');
  END;
END.
```

Related routines: _Arc, _Ellipse, _FloodFill, _LineTo, _Pie, _RemapAllPalette, _SetActivePage, _SetBkColor, _SetColor, _SetPixel, _SetTextColor, _SetTextCursor, _SetVisualPage, _SetWindow, _SetWriteMode

Halt   System

Ends program execution, returning an optional exit status value to the calling environment.

Syntax
PROCEDURE Halt[(*statusValue*: Word)];

Arguments
statusValue is the optional exit status value your program returns to the calling environment.

Notes
The DOS IF ERRORLEVEL command can test program exit status values, letting a batch file perform conditional processing based upon the success of your program.

Example
```
PROGRAM HaltCheck;

VAR
  index: Byte;   { index to command line arguments }

BEGIN
  IF (ParamCount < 1) THEN
    BEGIN
      Writeln('Insufficient command line');
      Halt(1);
    END
  ELSE
    FOR index := 1 TO ParamCount DO
      Writeln(ParamStr(index));
END.
```

Related routines: DosExitCode, Exec, Exit, Keep

Hi
System

Returns the byte value contained in the high-order byte of a Word or Integer value.

Syntax
FUNCTION Hi(*value*: <Integer *or* Word>): Byte;

Arguments
value is the Integer or Word expression from which Hi extracts the high-order byte.

Notes
The Swap function exchanges a Word or Integer value's high-order and low-order bytes.

Example
See DosVersion.

Related routines: Lo, Swap

HighVideo
Crt

Selects high-intensity video display for subsequent text output.

Syntax
PROCEDURE HighVideo;

Arguments
None.

Notes
QuickPascal supports both normal and high-intensity text display.

The color values 0 through 7 are low-intensity colors. The color values 8 through 15 are high-intensity colors. Selecting high-intensity video display for high-intensity colors has no effect.

Example

```
PROGRAM VideoIntensity;

USES
  Crt;  { contains video intensity routines }
BEGIN
  Writeln('Default intensity');
  HighVideo;
  Writeln('High intensity');
  LowVideo;
  Writeln('Low intensity');
  NormVideo;
  Writeln('Default intensity');
END.
```

Related routines: LowVideo, NormVideo, TextColor

_ImageSize   MSGraph

Returns the number of bytes required to store a graphics image.

Syntax
FUNCTION _ImageSize(*upperLeftx*, *upperLefty*, *lowerRightx*, *lowerRighty*: Integer): LongInt;

Arguments
upperLeftx and *upperLefty* are the *x* and *y* viewport coordinates of the upper left corner of the rectangle that bounds the image.

lowerRightx and *lowerRighty* are the *x* and *y* viewport coordinates of the lower right corner of the rectangle that bounds the image.

Notes

The number of bytes required to store an image differs depending upon the current graphics mode. _ImageSize lets your program determine during execution the correct buffer size.

The _GrStatus function returns the following status value for _ImageSize:

Status	Meaning
_GrNotInProperMode	Invalid video display mode

Example
See _GetImage.

Related routines: _GetImage, _GrStatus, _ImageSize_w, _ImageSize_wxy, _PutImage

_ImageSize_w   MSGraph

Returns the number of bytes required to store an image using window coordinates.

Syntax
FUNCTION _ImageSize_w(*upperLeftx*, *upperLefty*, *lowerRightx*, *lowerRighty*: Double): LongInt;

Arguments
upperLeftx and *upperLefty* are the window (floating-point) coordinates of the upper left corner of the rectangle that bounds the image.

lowerRightx and *lowerRighty* are the window (floating-point) coordinates of the lower right corner of the rectangle that bounds the image.

Notes
With the exception that _ImageSize_w uses window coordinates, it behaves identically to _ImageSize.

Related routines: _GetImage_w, _GrStatus, _ImageSize, _ImageSize_wxy, _PutImage_w

_ImageSize_wxy — MSGraph

Returns the number of bytes required to store a graphics image, using window coordinates.

Syntax
FUNCTION _ImageSize_wxy(VAR *upperLeftxy*,
  lowerRightxy: _WXYCoord): LongInt;

Arguments
upperLeftxy is a record containing the window coordinates of the upper left corner of the rectangle that bounds the image.

lowerLeftxy is a record containing the window coordinates of the lower right corner of the rectangle that bounds the image.

Notes
The MSGraph unit defines the record type _WXYCoord as follows:

```
_WXYCoord = RECORD
  wx: Double;   { window x coordinate }
  wy: Double;   { window y coordinate }
END;
```

With the exception that it uses window coordinates, _ImageSize_wxy behaves identically to _ImageSize.

Related routines: _GetImage_wxy, _GrStatus, _ImageSize, _ImageSize_w, _PutImage_w

Inc — System

Increments an ordinal variable by the specified amount.

Syntax
PROCEDURE Inc(VAR *ordinalVariable*: *<ordinal type>*
   [; *increment*: LongInt]);

Arguments
ordinalVariable is the variable to be incremented.

increment is the optional amount to be added to the ordinal variable. If you don't specify an increment, the default is 1.

Notes
Ordinal types include Boolean, Char, integer types, and subrange and enumerated types.

Incrementing an ordinal value by 1 is functionally equivalent to using the Succ function.

If your program increments an ordinal value past the last value in the type, a range error occurs. Using the {$R+} compiler directive, your program can test for this error.

Example
See Dec.

Related routines: Dec, First, Last, Ord, Pred, Succ

Insert   System

Places a substring within another string.

Syntax
PROCEDURE Insert(*sourceString*: *<string type>*;
   VAR *targetString*: *<string type>*; *insertIndex*: Integer);

Arguments
sourceString is the substring to be inserted.

targetString is the string into which Insert places the substring.

insertIndex is the character index in the target string at which the substring is placed.

Notes

If the resulting string length exceeds the target-string length, Insert truncates the string.

If the insert index exceeds the target-string length, Insert appends the substring.

Example

```
PROGRAM InsertWord;

VAR
  language: STRING;

BEGIN
  language := 'Microsoft Pascal';
  Insert('Quick', language, 11);
  Writeln(language);
END.
```

Related routines: Concat, Copy, Delete, Length, Pos, Str, Val

InsLine   Crt

Inserts a blank line at the row containing the cursor.

Syntax
PROCEDURE InsLine;

Arguments
None.

Notes

InsLine scrolls the line containing the cursor and all following lines down one line. The bottom window line disappears. The new line consists of blanks in the current background color.

Example

```pascal
PROGRAM InsertLine;

USES
  Crt;

VAR
  lineNumber: Byte;   { current line number }
  count: Byte;        { loop counter }
BEGIN
  ClrScr;
  Window(20, 10, 60, 20);
  FOR lineNumber := 1 TO 10 DO
    BEGIN
      FOR count := 1 TO 10 DO
        Write(lineNumber:3);
      Writeln;
    END;

  GotoXY(1, 5);
  Delay(5000);
  InsLine;
  Delay(5000);
  Writeln('  4 1/2   4 1/2   4 1/2   4 1/2');
  Delay(5000);
END.
```

Related routines: ClrEol, ClrScr, DelLine, GotoXY, TextBackground

Int   System

Truncates the fractional portion of a floating-point value.

Syntax
FUNCTION Int(value: *<real type>*): *<real type>*;

Arguments
value is the floating-point value to be truncated.

Notes

The Int function returns a floating-point value as a whole number, that is, with no digits to the right of the decimal point. The Int function differs from Trunc in that Int returns a floating-point value whereas Trunc returns an integer.

Example

```
PROGRAM IntPart;

BEGIN
  Writeln(Int(0.123456):5:2);
  Writeln(Int(1.234567):5:2);
  Writeln(Int(12.34567):5:2);
END.
```

Related routines: Frac, Round, Trunc

Intr
Dos

Invokes a BIOS interrupt service routine.

Syntax

PROCEDURE Intr(*interruptNumber*: Byte;
    VAR *registerValues*: Registers);

Arguments

interruptNumber is a byte value from 0 through 255 that specifies the desired interrupt.

registerValues is a record of type Registers that lets the program pass parameters to the interrupt service routine.

Notes

The DOS unit defines the record type Registers as follows:

```
Registers = RECORD
  CASE Integer OF
    0: (AX, BX, CX, DX, BP, SI, DI, DS, ES,
        Flags: Word);
    1: (AL, AH, BL, BH, CL, CH, DL, DH: Byte);
  END;
```

When called, Intr assigns to the corresponding hardware registers the values your program specifies. Next the routine initiates the desired interrupt and assigns the ending register contents back to the Registers record.

Do not use Intr with services that return a value in the SP or SS register.

Example

```
PROGRAM BIOSIntr;

USES
  Dos;  { contains Intr procedure }

VAR
  regs: Registers;

BEGIN
  { print the screen contents using interrupt 5 }
  Intr(5, regs);
END.
```

Related routines: GetIntVec, MsDos, SetIntVec

IOResult
System

Returns the status of the last I/O operation.

Syntax
FUNCTION IOResult: Word;

Arguments
None.

Notes
To trap I/O errors your program must disable and enable I/O checking using the {$I–} and {$I+} compiler directives.

The following table shows IOResult return values:

Value	Meaning
100	Disk read error. Program attempted to read past the end of a typed file.
101	Disk write error. Target disk is full.
102	File not assigned. A call to Reset, Rewrite, Append, Rename, or Erase used a file pointer not yet assigned to a file.
103	File not open. Program attempted an I/O operation on a closed file.
104	File not open for input. Program attempted a read or seek operation on a text file not open for input.
105	File not open for output. Program attempted a write operation on a text file not open for output.
106	Invalid numeric format. User entered an invalid data format for a Read or Readln statement.

Example

See Append.

Related routines: Append, BlockRead, BlockWrite, Close, Eof, Eoln, FileSize, Flush, Read, Readln, Seek, SeekEof, SeekEoln, Write, Writeln

Keep

Dos

Terminates a program but keeps it in memory as a TSR (terminate-and-stay-resident) program.

Syntax

PROCEDURE Keep(*exitStatus*: Word);

Arguments

exitStatus is the exit status value returned to the operating system or parent process.

Notes

Use the {$M} compiler directive to reduce the stack and heap sizes to their minimum values.

Do not run TSR programs from within the QuickPascal programming environment.

Related routines: DosExitCode, Exec, Exit, Halt

KeyPressed   Crt

Returns true if the user has pressed a key that has not yet been read.

Syntax
FUNCTION KeyPressed: Boolean;

Arguments
None.

Notes
If the keyboard buffer contains an unread key, KeyPressed returns true. If the keyboard buffer is empty, KeyPressed returns false.

KeyPressed ignores shift keys such as Shift, Alt, Ctrl, and NumLock.

After KeyPressed returns true, your program can use ReadKey to read the keystroke.

Example
See _Ellipse.

Related routines: Delay, ReadKey

Last   System

Returns the last value in a list of ordinal values.

Syntax
FUNCTION Last(value: <ordinal type>):
  <same type as argument>;

Argument
value is an ordinal type such as Integer, Boolean, and so on.

Notes
Ordinal types include Boolean, Char, integer types, and subrange and enumerated types.

Example
See First.

Related routines: Dec, First, Inc, Ord, Pred, Succ

Length
System

Returns the number of characters in a string.

Syntax
FUNCTION Length(*sourceStr*: <string type>): Integer;

Arguments
sourceStr is the string for which Length returns the current number of characters.

Notes
The Length function returns the current string length, not the declared length. To determine the declared length, use SizeOf.

Example
```
PROGRAM StringLengths;

BEGIN
  Writeln('QuickPascal contains ',
    Length('QuickPascal'), ' characters');
```

```
Writeln('ABC contains ', Length($FSTABC'),
  ' characters');
Writeln('The string '''' contains ', Length(''),
  ' characters');
END.
```

Related routines: Concat, Copy, Delete, Insert, Ord, Pos, SizeOf, Str, Val

_LineTo   MSGraph

Draws a line from the current graphics position to the specified *x* and *y* viewport coordinates.

Syntax
PROCEDURE _LineTo(*x*, *y*: Integer);

Arguments
x and *y* are the viewport coordinates of the line's ending point.

Notes
The current graphics position is the *x* and *y* coordinates of the last _MoveTo or _LineTo function.

_LineTo draws the line using the current color, line style, and write mode.

When _LineTo completes execution, it updates the current graphics position to the line's ending point.

The _GrStatus function returns the following status values for _LineTo:

Status	Meaning
_GrClipped	Line clipped to fit viewport
_GrNoOutput	No line drawn
_GrNotInProperMode	Invalid video mode display

Example

```
PROGRAM Lines;

USES
  MSGraph,  { contains graphics routines }
  Crt;      { contains the KeyPressed function }

VAR
  status: Integer;

BEGIN
  { set the video mode to 320 by 200 graphics }
  status := _SetVideoMode(_MRes4Color);

  { draw the center box }
  _MoveTo(130, 70);
  _LineTo(190, 70);   { top line }
  _LineTo(190, 130);  { right side }
  _LineTo(130, 130);  { bottom line }
  _LineTo(130, 70);   { left side }

  { draw the outer box }
  _MoveTo(120, 50);
  _LineTo(200, 50);   { top line }
  _MoveTo(210, 55);
  _LineTo(210, 145);  { right side }
  _MoveTo(200, 150);
  _LineTo(120, 150);  { bottom line }
  _MoveTo(110, 145);
  _LineTo(110, 55);   { left side }

  _SetTextPosition(23, 8);
  _OutText('Press any key to continue');

  WHILE (NOT KeyPressed) DO
    ;

  { restore the original video mode }
  status := _SetVideoMode(_DefaultMode);
END.
```

Related routines: _GrStatus, _LineTo_w, _MoveTo, _SetLineStyle, _SetWriteMode

_LineTo_w

MSGraph

Draws a line from the current graphics position to the specified window coordinates.

Syntax
PROCEDURE _LineTo_w(*realx*, *realy*: Double);

Arguments
realx and *realy* are the window (floating-point) coordinates of the line's ending point.

Notes
With the exception that it uses window coordinates, _LineTo_w behaves identically to _LineTo.

Related routines: _GrStatus, _LineTo, _MoveTo, _SetLineStyle, _SetWriteMode

Ln

System

Returns the natural logarithm of a floating-point value.

Syntax
FUNCTION Ln(*value*: <real type>): <real type>;

Arguments
value is the floating-point number for which Ln returns the natural logarithm.

Notes
A natural logarithm is a logarithm to the base *e*.

If the argument to Ln is less than or equal to 0, a run-time error occurs.

Example
See Exp.

Related routine: Exp

Lo
System

Returns the byte value contained in the low-order byte of a Word or Integer value.

Syntax
FUNCTION Lo(*value*: <Integer *or* Word >): Byte;

Arguments
value is the Integer or Word value from which Lo extracts the low-order byte.

Notes
The QuickPascal Swap function exchanges the values of a Word or Integer value's high-order and low-order bytes.

Example
See DosVersion.

Related routines: Hi, Swap

LowVideo
Crt

Selects low-intensity video display for subsequent text output.

Syntax
PROCEDURE LowVideo;

Arguments
None.

Notes

QuickPascal supports both normal and high-intensity text display.

The text color values 0 through 7 are low-intensity colors. The color values 8 through 15 are high-intensity colors. Selecting low-intensity video display for low-intensity colors has no effect.

Example
See HighVideo.

Related routines: HighVideo, NormVideo, TextColor

Mark
System

Records the address of the current top of the heap so that a future call to Release can free all allocated memory down to this point.

Syntax
PROCEDURE Mark(VAR *heapTop*: Pointer);

Arguments
heapTop is an untyped pointer to which Mark assigns the address of the current heap top.

Notes
The Release procedure frees all allocated memory above the heap address Mark saves. By using Mark and Release together, your program can quickly release dynamic memory.

Example
```
PROGRAM MarkHeap;

VAR
  heapTop: Pointer;
  ptr1, ptr2: Pointer;
```

(continued)

continued

```
BEGIN
  { mark the current heap position }
  Mark(heapTop);

  Writeln('Current heap space: ', MemAvail);

  IF (MaxAvail > 1000) THEN
    GetMem(ptr1, 1000);

  IF (MaxAvail > 5000) THEN
    GetMem(ptr2, 5000);

  Writeln('Heap space after allocation: ',
  MemAvail);

  { release allocated memory }
  Release(heapTop);

  Writeln('Heap space after release: ', MemAvail);
END.
```

Related routines: Addr, Dispose, FreeMem, GetMem, MaxAvail, MemAvail, New, Release, SizeOf

MaxAvail
System

Returns the size of the largest available block of heap space.

Syntax
FUNCTION MaxAvail: LongInt;

Arguments
None.

Notes
The procedures New and GetMem allocate memory from the heap. The MaxAvail function lets your program test first whether sufficient heap space exists.

QuickPascal provides the global variable HeapPtr, which always points to the top of the heap. The MaxAvail function returns either the largest block of available heap space in the free list or the size of the free memory heap above HeapPtr, whichever is larger.

The QuickPascal {$M} compiler directive lets your program adjust the amount of available heap space.

Example

```
PROGRAM AvailableHeapSpace;

VAR
  ptr1, ptr2, ptr3: Pointer;

BEGIN
  Writeln('Initial MemAvail: ', MemAvail,
  ' MaxAvail: ', MaxAvail);

  IF (MaxAvail > 5000) THEN
    BEGIN
      Writeln('Allocating 5000 bytes');
      GetMem(ptr1, 5000);
    END;
  Writeln('Current MemAvail: ', MemAvail,
  ' MaxAvail: ', MaxAvail);

  IF (MaxAvail > 10000) THEN
    BEGIN
      Writeln('Allocating 10000 bytes');
      GetMem(ptr2, 10000);
    END;
  Writeln('Current MemAvail: ', MemAvail,
  ' MaxAvail: ', MaxAvail);

  IF (MaxAvail > 1000) THEN
    BEGIN
      Writeln('Allocating 1000 bytes');
      GetMem(ptr3, 1000);
    END;
  Writeln('Current MemAvail: ', MemAvail,
  ' MaxAvail: ', MaxAvail);
```

(continued)

continued
```
  Writeln('Freeing 10000 bytes');
  FreeMem(ptr2, 10000);
  Writeln('Current MemAvail: ', MemAvail,
  ' MaxAvail: ', MaxAvail);

  Writeln('Freeing all allocated memory');
  FreeMem(ptr1, 5000);
  FreeMem(ptr3, 1000);
  Writeln('Current MemAvail: ', MemAvail,
  ' MaxAvail: ', MaxAvail);
END.
```

Related routines: Addr, Dispose, FreeMem, GetMem, Mark, MemAvail, New, Release, SizeOf

MemAvail
System

Returns the total amount of available heap space in the free list.

Syntax
FUNCTION MemAvail: LongInt;

Arguments
None.

Notes
QuickPascal uses a free list to manage areas in the heap that have been allocated by New or GetMem and later released by Dispose or FreeMem. The global variable FreePtr always points to the free list. The MemAvail function returns the total number of bytes that are available in the free list.

The QuickPascal {$M} compiler directive lets your program adjust the amount of available heap space.

Example
See MaxAvail.

Related routines: Addr, Dispose, FreeMem, GetMem, Mark, MaxAvail, New, Release, SizeOf

Member — System

Returns true if an object is a member of the specified class.

Syntax
FUNCTION Member(*objectVariable*: OBJECT;
    className: <class>): Boolean;

Arguments
objectVariable is the variable that Member tests for membership in the specified class.

className is the class that Member tests.

Notes
Membership in a class implies that an object understands the class methods as well as the methods of all the class ancestors.

Related routines: None.

MkDir — System

Creates a directory on the specified disk drive.

Syntax
PROCEDURE MkDir(*pathname*: <string type>);

Arguments
pathname is the DOS pathname of the new directory. It can contain a disk-drive letter and subdirectory path.

Notes

The MkDir procedure behaves identically to the DOS MKDIR command. The pathname must be a valid name and cannot already exist.

You can test MkDir's success by disabling I/O checking, using the {$I–} compiler directive, and then calling IOResult.

Example

```
PROGRAM MakeDirectory;

VAR
  directory: STRING;  { directory to create }

BEGIN
  Write('Enter name of directory to create: ');
  Readln(directory);

  {$I-} { disable I/O checking }
  MkDir(directory);
  {$I+} { enable I/O checking }

  IF (IOResult <> 0) THEN
    Writeln('Error creating ', directory)
  ELSE
    Writeln('directory ', directory, ' created');
END.
```

Related routines: ChDir, GetDir, IOResult, RmDir

Move   System

Copies values from one memory location to another.

Syntax
PROCEDURE Move(VAR *source, target*: <*any type*>;
   numBytes: Word);

Arguments
source is the memory location containing the data to be copied.

target is the destination memory location to which Move copies the data.

numBytes is the number of bytes to be copied.

Notes

The Move procedure does not perform range checking. It is possible, therefore, for Move to overwrite memory contents if your program calls it incorrectly.

Move is more efficient for array copies than a loop that assigns an element at a time.

Example

```
PROGRAM FastArrayCopy;

VAR
  a: ARRAY[1..100] OF Real;
  b: ARRAY[1..100] OF Real;
  index: Integer;  { index into the array }

BEGIN
  { initialize an array }
  FOR index := 1 TO 100 DO
    a[index] := Random;

  { perform a fast copy }
  Move(a, b, SizeOf(a));

  { display array values }
  FOR index := 1 TO 100 DO
    Writeln(a[index]:8:5, b[index]:10:5);
END.
```

Related routines: FillChar, SizeOf

_MoveTo   MSGraph

Moves the current graphics position to the specified *x* and *y* viewport coordinates.

Syntax

PROCEDURE _MoveTo(*x, y*: Integer);

Arguments

x and *y* are the viewport coordinates to which _MoveTo moves the current graphics position.

Notes

The _LineTo and _OutGText routines also change the current graphics position.

The _GrStatus function returns the following status value for _MoveTo:

Status	Meaning
_GrNotInValidMode	Invalid video display mode

Example

See _LineTo.

Related routines: _GrStatus, _LineTo, _MoveTo_w, _OutGText

_MoveTo_w   MSGraph

Moves the current graphics position to the specified window coordinates.

Syntax

PROCEDURE _MoveTo_w(*realx*, *realy*: Double);

Arguments

realx and *realy* are the window (floating-point) coordinates to which _MoveTo_w moves the current graphics position.

Notes

With the exception that _MoveTo_w uses window coordinates, _MoveTo_w behaves identically to _MoveTo.

Related routines: _GrStatus, _LineTo, _MoveTo, _OutGText

MsDos

Dos

Calls DOS interrupt 21H, passing the specified register values.

Syntax
PROCEDURE MsDos(VAR *registerValues*: Registers);

Arguments
registerValues is a record variable of type Registers that the program uses to pass parameters to the DOS system services.

Notes
The Dos unit defines the Registers record as follows:

```
Registers = RECORD
  CASE Integer OF
    0: (AX, BX, CX, DX, BP, SI, DI, DS, ES,
        Flags: Word);
    1: (AL, AH, BL, BH, CL, CH, DL, DH: Byte);
  END;
```

When called, MsDos assigns to the corresponding hardware registers the register values your program specifies. Next the procedure calls the DOS system service specified in the AH register. After the system service completes execution, MsDos assigns the ending register contents back to the registers variable.

Example

```
PROGRAM GetSystemDate;

USES
  Dos;   { contains MsDos and Registers }

VAR
  regs: Registers;

BEGIN
  WITH regs DO
```

(continued)

continued

```
    BEGIN
      AH := $2A;
      MsDos(regs);

      Writeln(DH, '/', DL, '/', CX);
    END;
END.
```

Related routines: Exec, Intr

New   System

Allocates a dynamic variable from the heap.

Syntax
PROCEDURE New(VAR *pointerVariable*: *<pointer type>*);

Arguments
pointerVariable is a pointer to the dynamic variable.

Notes
Do not intermix calls to GetMem and FreeMem with calls to New and Dispose. Doing so will make your program difficult to understand.

New cannot allocate a variable larger than 65,520 bytes. If the heap does not have sufficient space for the memory allocation, a run-time error occurs. Use the MaxAvail and MemAvail functions to determine the amount of available heap space.

When your program no longer requires the dynamic variable, release the corresponding heap space using Dispose.

Example
See Dispose.

Related routines: Addr, Dispose, FreeMem, GetMem, Mark, MaxAvail, MemAvail, Release, SizeOf

NormVideo — Crt

Returns text attributes to the original program start-up value.

Syntax
PROCEDURE NormVideo;

Arguments
None.

Notes
The NormVideo procedure restores text attributes to their original settings following calls to LowVideo and HighVideo.

Example
See HighVideo.

Related routines: HighVideo, LowVideo, TextBackground, TextColor

NoSound — Crt

Disables the sound emitted by the computer's built-in speaker.

Syntax
PROCEDURE NoSound;

Arguments
None.

Notes

The Sound procedure enables a tone from the computer's built-in speaker. The NoSound procedure disables the tone.

If your program generates a sound and does not invoke NoSound before ending, the sound remains in effect after the program ends.

Example
See Delay.

Related routines: Delay, KeyPressed, ReadKey, Sound

Odd
System

Returns true if a value is odd or false if the value is even.

Syntax
FUNCTION Odd(*value*: LongInt): Boolean;

Arguments
value is the number that Odd tests.

Notes
A whole number is odd if it cannot be evenly divided by 2.

Example
```
PROGRAM EvenOdd;

VAR
  i: Integer;  { loop counter }

BEGIN
  FOR i := 1 TO 100 DO
    IF (Odd(i)) THEN
      Writeln(i, ' is odd')
    ELSE
      Writeln(i, ' is even');
END.
```

Related routines: Abs, Round, Trunc

Ofs
System

Returns the offset address for a variable, function, or procedure.

Syntax
FUNCTION Ofs(*identifier*: <*variable, function, or procedure*>): Word;

Arguments
identifier is the variable, function, or procedure for which Ofs returns the offset address.

Notes
The IBM PC and PC-compatibles access memory locations using a 16-bit segment and a 16-bit offset address. The Ofs function returns an identifier's 16-bit offset address.

Example
```
PROGRAM SegmentOffset;

VAR
  intValue: Integer;   { declare integer variable }
  intPointer: ^Integer; { declare integer pointer }

BEGIN
  { assign intPointer the address of intValue }
  intPointer := @intValue;

  { display the address of intValue }
  Writeln('intValue--Segment: ', Seg(intValue),
    ' Offset: ', Ofs(intValue));

  { display segment and offset of pointer }
  Writeln('intPointer^--Segment: ',
    Seg(intPointer^), ' Offset: ',
    Ofs(intPointer^));

  { display address of pointer }
  Writeln('intPointer--Segment: ', Seg(intPointer),
    ' Offset: ', Ofs(intPointer));
END.
```

Related routines: Addr, CSeg, DSeg, Ptr, Seg, SPtr, SSeg

Ord System

Returns a scalar type's ordinal value.

Syntax
FUNCTION Ord(*ordinalValue*: <*ordinal type*>): LongInt;

Arguments
ordinalValue is the value for which Ord returns the ordinality.

Notes
A scalar type is any QuickPascal type consisting of a finite set of ordered elements of a type such as Char, Integer, Byte, an enumerated type, and so on.

QuickPascal begins the ordinality of enumerated types with zero. Consider the following type:

```
TYPE
  Colors = (Red, Green, Blue);
```

The Ord function returns the following values:

- Ord(Red) returns 0
- Ord(Green) returns 1
- Ord(Blue) returns 2

For ASCII characters, the Ord function is the inverse of Chr. The Chr function converts a value to its corresponding ASCII character. The Ord function converts an ASCII character to its corresponding numeric value.

Related routines: Chr, Dec, First, Inc, Last, Pred, Succ

_OutGText
MSGraph

Displays text in graphics mode using program-selected fonts.

Syntax
PROCEDURE _OutGText(*text*: CSTRING);

Arguments
text is a variable of type CSTRING that contains the text _OutGText is to display.

Notes
The _OutGText procedure works only in graphics mode.

_OutGText displays text at the current graphics position using the current font and color. It ignores carriage returns, linefeeds, and tabs.

_SetGTextVector lets your program define the rotation angle _OutGText uses to display text.

The _GrStatus function returns the following status values for _OutGText:

Status	Meaning
_GrClipped	Output clipped to fit viewport
_GrNoOutput	No image drawn
_GrNotInProperMode	Invalid video display mode

Example
See _SetFont.

Related routines: _GetGTextExtent, _GetGTextVector, _GrStatus, _MoveTo, _RegisterFonts, _SetColor, _SetFont, _SetGTextVector

_OutMem — MSGraph

Displays a text string in either text mode or graphics mode.

Syntax
PROCEDURE _OutMem(*text*: CSTRING;
   textLength: Integer);

Arguments
text is the character string _OutMem displays.

textLength is the number of characters _OutMem is to display.

Notes
The _OutMem procedure displays characters at the current text position in the current text color.

The _OutMem procedure does not translate carriage returns, linefeeds, or tab characters. Instead, _OutMem displays their corresponding ASCII values.

The _OutMem procedure does not perform range checking. If the string's actual length is less than the number of characters _OutMem is to display, _OutMem displays the values in successive memory locations.

Related routines: _OutText, _OutGText, _SetTextColor, _SetTextPosition

_OutText — MSGraph

Displays a text string in either text mode or graphics mode.

Syntax
PROCEDURE _OutText(*text*: CSTRING);

Arguments
text is the character string _OutText sends to the screen.

Notes

The _OutText procedure displays a text string at the current text position using the current text color.

The _OutText procedure translates the carriage return and linefeed characters, advancing the cursor appropriately. The _OutText procedure does not translate tab characters.

Example
See _Ellipse_w.

Related routines: _OutGText, _OutMem, _SetTextColor, _SetTextPosition, _SetTextWindow

PackTime   Dos

Converts the date and time information stored in a record of type DateTime into a LongInt value that contains the date and time in a compressed format.

Syntax
PROCEDURE PackTime(VAR *dateTimeRecord*: DateTime; VAR *packedDateTime*: LongInt);

Arguments
dateTimeRecord is a record of type DateTime that contains the date and time that PackTime is to compress.

packedDateTime is the LongInt variable to which PackTime assigns the compressed time.

Notes
The Dos unit defines the DateTime record as follows:

```
DateTime = RECORD
  Year, Month, Day, Hour, Min, Sec: Word;
END;
```

The compressed date and time is stored in the LongInt value as shown in Figure 2 on the following page.

Bit	31	30	29	28	27	26	25	24	23	22	21	20	19	18	17	16	15	14	13	12	11	10	9	8	7	6	5	4	3	2	1	0
Value	Year							Month				Day					Hour					Minute						Second				
Range	1–99							1–12				1–31					0–23					0–59						0–59				

Figure 2. *The packed time format.*

Related routines: FindFirst, FindNext, GetDate, GetFTime, GetTime, SetDate, SetFTime, SetTime, UnpackTime

ParamCount System

Returns the number of command line parameters with which the program was executed.

Syntax
FUNCTION ParamCount: Word;

Arguments
None.

Notes
ParamCount returns 0 if no command line arguments are present.

The QuickPascal Run/Debug option on the Options menu lets you define the command line that QuickPascal uses in the QuickPascal environment.

Example
```
PROGRAM ShowCommandLine;

VAR
   index: Byte;       { command line argument index }
   numParams: Byte;   { number of parameters }
```

```
BEGIN
  numParams := ParamCount;

  FOR index := 1 TO NumParams DO
    Writeln(ParamStr(index));
END.
```

Related routine: ParamStr

ParamStr   System

Returns a specific command line parameter.

Syntax
FUNCTION ParamStr(*parameterIndex*: Word): STRING;

Arguments
parameterIndex is the index to the desired command line parameter.

Notes
Consider the following command line:

`SOMEPROG A B C`

The ParamCount function returns the value 3, and the index values 1 through 3 direct ParamStr to return the following:

- ParamStr(1) returns *A*
- ParamStr(2) returns *B*
- ParamStr(3) returns *C*

If you are using MS-DOS version 3.0 or later, the call *ParamStr(0)* returns the program's complete pathname.

Example
See ParamCount.

Related routine: ParamCount

Pi

System

Returns the value of the mathematical symbol π (pi).

Syntax
FUNCTION Pi: Real;

Arguments
None.

Notes
If your program uses the {$N+} compiler directive to generate 8087 code, the Pi function returns the value 3.1415926535897932383.

If your program does not generate 8087 code, the Pi function returns the value 3.14159265358979.

Example
See Cos.

Related routines: Abs, Sqrt

_Pie

MSGraph

Draws a pie-shaped wedge on the screen in graphics mode.

Syntax
PROCEDURE _Pie(*fillControl, upperLeftx, upperLefty, lowerRightx, lowerRighty, startx, starty, stopx, stopy*: Integer);

Arguments
fillControl specifies whether _Pie fills the pie shape or only draws the border. The MSGraph unit defines two constants for fill control.

Constant	Meaning
_GFillInterior	Fill the pie shape.
_GBorder	Draw the pie-shaped border only.

upperLeftx and *upperLefty* are the *x* and *y* viewport coordinates of the upper left corner of the rectangle that bounds the elliptical arc.

lowerRightx and *lowerRighty* are the *x* and *y* viewport coordinates of the lower right corner of the rectangle that bounds the elliptical arc.

startx and *starty* are the *x* and *y* viewport coordinates of the arc's start vector.

stopx and *stopy* are the *x* and *y* viewport coordinates of the arc's stop vector.

Notes

_Pie draws the pie-shaped wedge using logical (viewport) screen coordinates.

The rectangle that bounds the ellipse defines its shape and size. The arc is drawn counterclockwise along the ellipse, beginning at the start vector and ending at the stop vector.

Upon completion of the _Pie procedure, the _GrStatus function returns the following status values:

Status	Meaning
_GrClipped	Wedge clipped to fit viewport
_GrInsufficientMemory	Not enough memory to complete operation
_GrInvalidParameter	Invalid parameter in call to _Pie
_GrNoOutput	No wedge drawn
_GrNotInProperMode	Invalid video display mode

Example

```
PROGRAM PieChart;

USES
  MSGraph,  { contains graphics routines }
  Crt;      { contains the KeyPressed function }
```

(continued)

continued

```
VAR
  status: Integer;

BEGIN
  { set the video mode to 320 by 200 graphics }
  status := _SetVideoMode(_MRes4Color);

  _Pie(_GBorder,
    100, 50, 200, 150, 150, 50, 100, 100);
  _Pie(_GBorder,
    100, 50, 200, 150, 100, 100, 180, 130);
  _Pie(_GFillInterior,
    110, 40, 210, 140, 190, 120, 160, 50);

  _SetTextPosition(23, 8);
  _OutText('Press any key to continue');

  WHILE (NOT KeyPressed) DO
    ;

  { restore the original video mode }
  status := _SetVideoMode(_DefaultMode);
END.
```

Related routines: _Arc, _Ellipse, _Pie_wxy, _Rectangle, _SetFillMask

_Pie_wxy

MSGraph

Draws a pie-shaped wedge on the screen in graphics mode, using window coordinates.

Syntax
PROCEDURE _Pie_wxy(*fillControl*: Integer;
    VAR *upperLeftxy*, *lowerRightxy*, *startxy*, *stopxy*:
    _WXYCoord);

Arguments
fillControl specifies whether _Pie_wxy fills the pie shape or only draws the border. The MSGraph unit defines two constants for fill control.

Part III: QuickPascal Functions and Procedures 171

Constant	Meaning
_GFillInterior	Fill the pie shape.
_GBorder	Draw the border only.

upperLeftxy contains the *x* and *y* window coordinates of the upper left corner of the rectangle that bounds the ellipse.

lowerRightxy contains the *x* and *y* window coordinates of the lower right corner of the rectangle that bounds the ellipse.

startxy contains the *x* and *y* window coordinates of the arc's start vector.

stopxy contains the *x* and *y* window coordinates of the arc's stop vector.

Notes

The MSGraph unit defines the record type _WXYCoord as follows:

```
_WXYCoord = RECORD
  wx: Double;   { window x coordinate }
  wy: Double;   { window y coordinate }
END;
```

With the exception that _Pie_wxy uses window coordinates, it behaves identically to _Pie.

Example

See _Ellipse_w.

Related routines: _Arc_wxy, _Ellipse_wxy, _Pie, _Rectangle_wxy, _SetFillMask

_Polygon   MSGraph

Draws a polygon in graphics mode.

Syntax

PROCEDURE _Polygon(*fillControl*: Integer; VAR *points*; *numPoints*: Integer);

Arguments

fillControl specifies whether _Polygon fills the polygon, using the current fill color and pattern, or simply draws the polygon's border. The MSGraph unit defines two fill-control constants:

Constant	Meaning
_GFillInterior	Fill the polygon.
_GBorder	Draw the polygon border only.

points is an array of type _XYCoord that contains the polygon vertices.

numPoints specifies the number of vertices in the polygon array.

Notes

The MSGraph unit defines the type _XYCoord as follows:

```
_XYCoord = RECORD
  xcoord: Integer;
  ycoord: Integer;
END;
```

Upon completion of the _Polygon procedure, the _GrStatus function returns the following error status values:

Status	Meaning
_GrNotInProperMode	Invalid video display mode
_GrInvalidParameter	Invalid parameter in call to _Polygon
_GrInsufficientMemory	Not enough memory to complete operation
_GrNoOutput	No polygon drawn
_GrClipped	Polygon clipped to fit in viewport

Example

```
PROGRAM FillPolygon;
USES
  MSGraph,  { contains graphics routines }
  Crt;      { contains the KeyPressed function }

VAR
  status: Integer;
  points: ARRAY[1..5] OF _XYCoord;
```

```
BEGIN
  { set the video mode to 320 by 200 graphics }
  status := _SetVideoMode(_MRes4Color);

  points[1].xcoord := 100; points[1].ycoord := 80;
  points[2].xcoord := 150; points[2].ycoord := 50;
  points[3].xcoord := 250; points[3].ycoord := 80;
  points[4].xcoord := 165; points[4].ycoord := 150;
  points[5].xcoord := 120; points[5].ycoord := 120;

  _Polygon(_GFillInterior, points, 5);

  _SetTextPosition(23, 8);
  _OutText('Press any key to continue');

  WHILE (NOT KeyPressed) DO
    ;

  { restore the original video mode }
  status := _SetVideoMode(_DefaultMode);
END.
```

Related routines: _GrStatus, _Polygon_wxy, _SetFillMask, _SetLineStyle

_Polygon_wxy   MSGraph

Draws a polygon in graphics mode using window coordinates.

Syntax
PROCEDURE _Polygon_wxy(*fillControl*: Integer; VAR *points*; *numPoints*: Integer);

Arguments
fillControl specifies whether _Polygon_wxy fills the polygon, using the current fill color and pattern, or simply draws the polygon's border. The MSGraph unit defines two fill-control constants.

Constant	Meaning
_GFillInterior	Fill the polygon.
_GBorder	Draw the polygon border only.

points is an array of type _WXYCoord that contains the polygon vertices.

numPoints specifies the number of vertices in the polygon array.

Notes

The MSGraph unit defines the type _WXYCoord as follows:

```
_WXYCoord = RECORD
  wx: Double;   { window x coordinate }
  wy: Double;   { window y coordinate }
END;
```

With the exception that _Polygon_wxy uses window coordinates, it behaves functionally the same as _Polygon does.

Related routines: _GrStatus, _Polygon, _SetFillMask, _SetLineStyle

Pos   System

Returns the starting character index of a substring within a string.

Syntax

FUNCTION Pos(*subString, sourceString*: <*string type*>):
   Byte;

Arguments

subString is the character string Pos searches for.

sourceString is the character string that Pos examines for the substring.

Notes

If Pos locates the substring within the source string, Pos returns the substring's starting index. If Pos doesn't locate the substring, Pos returns 0.

Pos does not consider uppercase letters and lowercase letters to be equivalent.

Example

```
PROGRAM SubstringPos;

VAR
  language: STRING;
  programName: STRING;
  index: Integer;

BEGIN
  language := 'QuickPascal';
  programName := 'SubstringPos';

  { look for Pascal in both strings }
  index := Pos('Pascal', language);
  Writeln('Looking for Pascal in the string ',
    language,'; the index value is ', index);

  index := Pos('Pascal', programName);
  Writeln('Looking for Pascal in the string ',
    programName,'; the index value is ', index);

  { look for the letter P in both strings }
  index := Pos('P', language);
  Writeln('Looking for P in the string ',
    language,'; the index value is ', index);
  index := Pos('P', programName);
  Writeln('Looking for P in the string ',
    programName,'; the index value is ', index);
END.
```

Related routines: Concat, Copy, Delete, Insert, Length, Str, Val

Pred
System

Returns an ordinal value's preceding value.

Syntax
FUNCTION Pred(*ordinalValue*: <*ordinal type*>):
   <*same type as argument*>;

Arguments
ordinalValue is the ordinal value for which Pred returns the predecessor.

Notes
Ordinal types include Boolean, Char, integer types, and subrange and enumerated types.

If you use Pred to return the ordinal before the first ordinal, a range error occurs.

Example
See First.

Related routines: First, Last, Ord, Succ

Ptr
System

Creates a pointer value from a segment and offset.

Syntax
FUNCTION Ptr(*segment*, *offset*: Word): Pointer;

Arguments
segment is a 16-bit segment address.

offset is a 16-bit offset address.

Notes
After your program creates a pointer, the program can use the caret operator (^) to access the value at the memory

location to which the pointer refers. Because the pointer is untyped, the value must be typecast before it can be used.

Related routines: Addr, CSeg, DSeg, Hi, Lo, New, Ofs, Seg, SPtr, SSeg

_PutImage   MSGraph

Displays a previously stored graphics image.

Syntax
PROCEDURE _PutImage(x, y: Integer; VAR *image*;
  displayVerb: Integer);

Arguments
x and *y* are the viewport coordinates at which _PutImage places the upper left corner of the rectangle containing the image.

image is the buffer containing the graphics image stored by _GetImage.

displayVerb tells _PutImage how to display the image. The MSGraph unit defines the following display verbs:

Verb	Result
_GAND	Displays the image over existing pixels. The final image is a logical AND of the image pixels and current screen contents.
_GOR	Displays the image over existing pixels. The final image is the logical OR of the image pixels and current screen contents.
_GPRESET	Places the image on the screen, overwriting existing pixels. _PutImage inverts each pixel in the image saved by _GetImage.
_GPSET	Places the image on the screen, overwriting existing pixels. _PutImage displays each pixel exactly as it was saved by _GetImage.
_GXOR	Displays the image over existing pixels. The final image is an exclusive OR of the image and the current screen contents.

Notes

The _GetImage and _PutImage functions work together, letting your program move objects on the screen display.

Upon completion of _PutImage, the _GrStatus function returns the following values:

Status	Meaning
_GrError	General graphics error
_GrInvalidImageBuffer	Invalid graphics image in buffer
_GrInvalidParameter	Invalid parameter in call to _PutImage
_GrNotInProperMode	Invalid video display mode

Example
See _GetImage.

Related routines: _GetImage, _GrStatus, _ImageSize, _PutImage_w

_PutImage_w MSGraph

Displays a previously stored graphics image, using window coordinates.

Syntax
PROCEDURE _PutImage_w(*realx*, *realy*: Double;
  VAR *image*; *displayVerb*: Integer);

Arguments

realx and *realy* are the *x* and *y* window coordinates at which _PutImage_w places the upper left corner of the rectangle that bounds the image.

image is the buffer containing the graphics image previously stored by _GetImage_w.

displayVerb tells _PutImage_w how to display the image.

Notes
With the exception that _PutImage_w uses window coordinates, it behaves identically to _PutImage.

Related routines: _GetImage_w, _GrStatus, _ImageSize_w, _PutImage

Random   System

Returns a "random" value from QuickPascal's random-number generator.

Syntax
FUNCTION Random[(*integerRange*: Word)]:
   <Real *or* Integer>;

Arguments
integerRange is a positive integer value that specifies the upper limit of random values (0 through 65,535).

Notes
The QuickPascal random-number generator is actually a pseudorandom-number generator. Each time your program begins, Random returns the same set of numbers. To initialize the random-number seed to a different value, use the Randomize function.

The Random function generates real values in the range 0.0 to 1.0. For integer values, the maximum range is 0 to 65,535. By specifying an upper limit, your program can control the range of random values Random returns.

Example
```
PROGRAM RandomNumbers;

VAR
   i: Integer;    { counter variable }
```

(continued)

continued
```
BEGIN
  Randomize;

  Writeln('Integer      Real');
  FOR i := 1 TO 10 DO
    Writeln(Random(65535):5, Random:15:5);
END.
```

Related routine: Randomize

Randomize   System

Initializes the random-number generator.

Syntax
PROCEDURE Randomize;

Arguments
None.

Notes
The QuickPascal random-number generator is actually a pseudorandom-number generator. By default, each time your program begins, it generates the same set of random numbers. QuickPascal generates the same set of random numbers to let your program generate a predictable set of numbers for testing.

To generate a different set of random values, your program must change the seed value Random uses to generate the values. The Randomize procedure does so in an unpredictable manner.

Example
See Random.

Related routine: Random

Read

System

Reads one or more values from a file or device.

Syntax
PROCEDURE Read([VAR *filePointer*: <*text or typed file*>;]
   VAR *variable1*: <*simple or component type*> [,...]);

Arguments
filePointer is an optional file pointer. If the file pointer is present, Read gets input from the corresponding file.

variable1 receives the first value Read gets from the file. To specify multiple variables, separate the variables with commas.

Notes
If the call to Read does not include a file pointer, Read performs keyboard input unless DOS is redirecting input because of the redirection operator.

For text-file input, Read treats a Ctrl+Z as an end-of-file marker except when the Crt unit is used. If your program is using the Crt unit, the CheckEOF variable is set to true when the end of the file is reached.

For keyboard input, Read differs from Readln in that if the user types in more values than Read has variables to read, Read buffers the excess values for the next Read statement. Readln, on the other hand, ignores the excess values.

Example
```
PROGRAM ShowSongFile;

TYPE
  Songs = RECORD
    title: STRING;         { song title }
    group: STRING;         { band name }
    currentlyOwn: Boolean; { true if owned }
    albumName: STRING;     { record title }
  END;
```

(continued)

continued

```
VAR
  song: Songs;
  inputFile: FILE OF Songs;  { song input file }
BEGIN
  Assign(inputFile, 'SONGS.DAT');

  {$I-} { disable I/O checking }
  Reset(inputFile);
  {$I+} { enable I/O checking }

  IF (IOResult <> 0) THEN
    Writeln('Error opening SONGS.DAT')
  ELSE
    BEGIN
      WHILE (NOT Eof(inputFile)) DO
        WITH song DO
          BEGIN
            Read(inputFile, song);
            Writeln(title);
            Writeln(group);
            Writeln(currentlyOwn);
            Writeln(albumName);
            Writeln;
          END;
      Close(inputFile);
    END;
END.
```

Related routines: Assign, Eof, IOResult, ReadKey, Readln, Reset, SeekEof, SeekEoln

ReadKey   Crt

Reads and returns a character from the keyboard without echoing the character.

Syntax
FUNCTION ReadKey: Char;

Arguments

None.

Notes

If the keyboard buffer is empty, ReadKey waits for the user to press a key. If the user presses a special-purpose key, such as a function key, ReadKey returns the null character. To determine which key was pressed, call ReadKey a second time and Readkey will return the key's scan code.

Example

See _DisplayCursor.

Related routines: KeyPressed, Read, Readln

Readln
System

Reads a line of text from a text file or assigns values to variables read from the keyboard.

Syntax

PROCEDURE Readln([VAR *filePointer*: Text;]
  [VAR *variable1*: <*simple type*>; [, ...]]);

Arguments

filePointer is an optional text-file pointer from which Readln reads text input. If none is specified, Readln reads input from the keyboard.

variable1 is the first variable to which Readln assigns a value read. The variable can be any simple type except Boolean. To specify multiple variables, separate the variables with commas.

Notes

If the call to Readln does not include a file pointer, Readln performs keyboard input unless DOS is redirecting input because of the redirection operator.

For text-file input, Readln treats a Ctrl+Z as an end-of-file marker except when the Crt unit is used. If your program is using the Crt unit, the CheckEOF variable will be set to true when the end of the file is reached.

For keyboard input, Readln differs from Read in that if the user types in more values than Readln has variables to read, Readln ignores the additional values. The Read procedure, on the other hand, buffers these values for the next Read statement.

Example
See Append.

Related routines: Assign, Eof, IOResult, Read, ReadKey, Reset, SeekEof, SeekEoln

_Rectangle   MSGraph

Draws a rectangle on the screen in graphics mode.

Syntax
PROCEDURE Rectangle(*fillControl*, *upperLeftx*, *upperLefty*, *lowerRightx*, *lowerRighty*: Integer);

Arguments
fillControl specifies whether _Rectangle fills the rectangle using the current fill color and pattern or simply draws the rectangle's border. The MSGraph unit defines two fill-control constants.

Constant	Meaning
_GFillInterior	Fill the rectangle.
_GBorder	Draw the rectangle's border only.

upperLeftx and *upperLefty* are the *x* and *y* viewport coordinates of the rectangle's upper left corner.

lowerRightx and *lowerRighty* are the *x* and *y* viewport coordinates of the rectangle's lower right corner.

Notes

Upon completion of the _Rectangle procedure, the _GrStatus function returns the following status values:

Status	Meaning
_GrClipped	Rectangle clipped to fit viewport
_GrInvalidParameter	Invalid parameter in call to _Rectangle
_GrNoOutput	No rectangle drawn
_GrNotInProperMode	Invalid video display mode

Example

```
PROGRAM TwoBoxes;

USES
  MSGraph,   { contains graphics routines }
  Crt;       { contains the KeyPressed function }

VAR
  status: Integer;

BEGIN
  { set the video mode to 320 by 200 graphics }
  status := _SetVideoMode(_MRes4Color);

  { draw the rectangle (border only) }
  _Rectangle(_GBorder, 55, 50, 130, 150);

  { draw the filled rectangle }
  _Rectangle(_GFillInterior, 180, 50, 255, 150);

  _SetTextPosition(23, 8);
  _OutText('Press any key to continue');

  WHILE (NOT KeyPressed) DO
    ;

  { restore the original video mode }
  status := _SetVideoMode(_DefaultMode);
END.
```

Related routines: _Rectangle_w, _Rectangle_wxy, _SetColor, _SetLineStyle, _SetFillMask, _SetWriteMode

_Rectangle_w   MSGraph

Draws a rectangle on the screen in graphics mode using window coordinates.

Syntax
PROCEDURE _Rectangle_w(*fillControl*: Integer;
  upperLeftx, upperLefty, lowerRightx, lowerRighty:
  Double);

Arguments
fillControl specifies whether _Rectangle_w fills the rectangle using the current fill color and pattern or simply draws the rectangle's border. The MSGraph unit defines two fill-control constants.

Constant	Meaning
_GFillInterior	Fill the rectangle.
_GBorder	Draw the rectangle's border only.

upperLeftx and *upperLefty* are the *x* and *y* window coordinates of the rectangle's upper left corner.

lowerRightx and *lowerRighty* are the *x* and *y* window coordinates of the rectangle's lower right corner.

Notes
With the exception that _Rectangle_w uses window coordinates, it functions identically to _Rectangle.

Example
See _Ellipse_w.

Related routines: _Rectangle, _Rectangle_wxy, _SetColor, _SetFillMask, _SetLineStyle, _SetWindow, _SetWriteMode

_Rectangle_wxy — MSGraph

Draws a rectangle on the screen in graphics mode using window coordinates.

Syntax
PROCEDURE _Rectangle_wxy(*fillControl*: Integer;
  VAR *upperLeftxy*, *lowerRightxy*: _WXYCoord);

Arguments
fillControl specifies whether _Rectangle_wxy fills the rectangle using the current fill color and pattern or simply draws the rectangle's border. The MSGraph unit defines two fill-control constants.

Constant	Meaning
_GFillInterior	Fill the rectangle.
_GBorder	Draw the rectangle's border only.

upperLeftxy is a record of type _WXYCoord containing the *x* and *y* window coordinates of the rectangle's upper left corner.

lowerRightxy is a record of type _WXYCoord containing the *x* and *y* window coordinates of the rectangle's lower right corner.

Notes
The MSGraph unit defines the type _WXYCoord as follows:

```
_WXYCoord = RECORD
  wx: Double;   { window x coordinate }
  wy: Double;   { window y coordinate }
END;
```

With the exception that _Rectangle_wxy uses records of type _WXYCoord and window coordinates, it functions identically to _Rectangle.

Related routines: _Rectangle, _Rectangle_w, _SetColor, _SetFillMask, _SetLineStyle, _SetWindow, _SetWriteMode

_RegisterFonts
MSGraph

Registers the font contained in the specified file for font-based graphics output.

Syntax
FUNCTION _RegisterFonts(*pathname*: CSTRING): Integer;

Arguments
pathname is the complete DOS pathname to the file containing the font to register. If the pathname contains wildcard characters, _RegisterFonts will register all font files that match the file specification.

Notes
QuickPascal font files have the extension FON. Before your program can access a font, the font must be registered.

If successful, _RegisterFont returns the number of fonts currently registered. If an error occurs, _RegisterFont returns a negative value:

Value	Meaning
−1	File or directory not found
−2	Invalid font file
−3	Damaged font file
−4	Insufficient memory for font registration

Upon completion of the _RegisterFonts function, the _GrStatus function returns the following status values:

Status	Meaning
_GrCorruptedFontFile	One or more of the font files was damaged.
_GrFontFileNotFound	The specified directory or filename is invalid.
_GrInsufficientMemory	The system has insufficient memory to create the font-registration data structures.
_GrInvalidFontFile	The specified font file is not valid.

Example
See _SetFont.

Related routines: _GetFontInfo, _GetGTextExtent, _GrStatus, _OutGText, _SetFont, _SetGTextVector, _UnRegisterFonts

Release   System

Releases all memory previously allocated from the heap that resides above the heap location flagged by the Mark routine.

Syntax
PROCEDURE Release(VAR *heapMark*: Pointer);

Arguments
heapMark is a pointer to the top of the heap set by the Mark procedure.

Notes
The Mark and Release procedures let your program quickly release dynamic memory locations back to the heap.

When Release completes execution, the allocated heap memory above the specified heap pointer is released back to the heap. Variables that point to these locations maintain their current values but should not be used until new memory is allocated for their use.

Example
See Mark.

Related routines: Addr, Dispose, FreeMem, GetMem, Mark, MaxAvail, MemAvail, New, SizeOf

_RemapAllPalette — MSGraph

Reassigns all colors on the color palette.

Syntax
PROCEDURE _RemapAllPalette(VAR *newPalette*);

Arguments
newPalette is an array of LongInt values that contains the desired color palette.

Notes
The color palette defines the colors your program can access. The default EGA palette contains the following color values:

Color Value	Color	Color Value	Color
0	Black	8	Gray
1	Blue	9	Light blue
2	Green	10	Light green
3	Cyan	11	Light cyan
4	Red	12	Light red
5	Magenta	13	Light magenta
6	Brown	14	Yellow
7	White	15	Bright white

After your program uses _RemapAllPalette to change color values, all objects previously drawn using the modified color values change automatically.

To change one color value, your program should call _RemapPalette. To change several palette colors, your program should call _RemapAllPalette.

Upon completion of the _RemapAllPalette procedure, the _GrStatus function returns the following status values:

Status	Meaning
_GrError	General graphics error
_GrInvalidParameter	Invalid array argument in call to _RemapAllPalette

Example

```pascal
PROGRAM RemapPalette;

USES
  MSGraph,  { contains graphics routines }
  Crt;      { contains KeyPressed and ReadKey }

CONST
  newPalette: ARRAY[1..16] OF LongInt = (_Black,
    _Red, _White, _Cyan, _Red, _Magenta, _Brown,
    _White, _Gray, _LightBlue, _LightGreen,
    _LightCyan, _LightRed, _LightMagenta, _Yellow,
    _BrightWhite);

VAR
  status: Integer;
  buffer: Char;
  count: Integer;

BEGIN
  { set the EGA video mode to 320 by 200 graphics }
  status := _SetVideoMode(_MRes16Color);

  _SetTextPosition(23, 8);
  _OutText('Press any key to continue');

  { draw the rectangles on the screen }
  FOR count := 1 TO 15 DO
    BEGIN
      _SetColor(count);
      _Rectangle(_GFillInterior, 60 + (10 * count),
        10, 10 * count + 70, 150);
    END;

  { wait for the user to press a key }
  buffer := ReadKey;

  { change the color palette }
  _RemapAllPalette(newPalette);

  WHILE (NOT KeyPressed) DO
    ;

  { restore the original video mode }
  status := _SetVideoMode(_DefaultMode);
END.
```

Related routines: _GrStatus, _RemapPalette, _SelectPalette, _SetBkColor, _SetColor

_RemapPalette   MSGraph

Changes one color on the EGA color palette.

Syntax
FUNCTION _RemapPalette(*colorIndex*: Integer;
    colorValue: LongInt): LongInt;

Arguments
colorIndex is the palette index of the color to change.

colorValue is a LongInt value containing the value of the desired color.

Notes
The MSGraph unit defines the following color constants: _Black, _Blue, _Green, _Cyan, _Red, _Magenta, _Brown, _White, _Gray, _LightBlue, _LightGreen, _LightCyan, _LightRed, _LightMagenta, _Yellow, and _BrightWhite.

The Notes section for the _RemapAllPalette function lists the default EGA palette colors.

Upon completion of the _RemapPalette procedure, the _GrStatus function returns the following status values:

Status	Meaning
_GrError	General graphics error
_GrInvalidParameter	Invalid parameter in call to _RemapPalette

When your program changes a color using _RemapPalette, objects currently drawn using the modified color change color instantly. You can change palette values to change an object's color without having to redraw the object.

Example

```pascal
PROGRAM RemapPalette;

USES
  MSGraph,  { contains graphics routines }
  Crt;      { contains KeyPressed and ReadKey }

VAR
  status: Integer;
  buffer: Char;
  count: Integer;
  oldColor: LongInt;

BEGIN
  { set the EGA video mode to 320 by 200 graphics }
  status := _SetVideoMode(_MRes16Color);

  _SetTextPosition(23, 8);
  _OutText('Press any key to continue');

  { draw the rectangles on the screen }
  FOR count := 1 TO 15 DO
    BEGIN
      _SetColor(count);
      _Rectangle(_GFillInterior, 60 + (10 * count),
        10, 10 * count + 70, 150);
    END;

  { wait for the user to press a key }
  buffer := ReadKey;

  { change the color red to blue }
  oldColor := _RemapPalette(4, _Blue);

  WHILE (NOT KeyPressed) DO
    ;

  { restore the original video mode }
  status := _SetVideoMode(_DefaultMode);
END.
```

Related routines: _GrStatus, _RemapAllPalette, _SelectPalette, _SetColor

Rename
System

Changes the name of a file on disk.

Syntax
PROCEDURE Rename(VAR *filePointer*: <file type>;
 filename: <string type>);

Arguments
filePointer is a file pointer previously assigned (by Assign) to the filename that is to be changed.

filename is a character string containing the desired filename. The character string cannot contain a directory path or drive name.

Notes
The Rename procedure behaves as the DOS RENAME command does. Rename cannot move a file to a different drive or directory.

If Rename cannot rename the file, an I/O error occurs. You can trap I/O errors by disabling I/O checking and testing the IOResult function.

Example
```
PROGRAM MyRename;

VAR
  inputFile: Text;
  sourceFile: STRING;
  targetFile: STRING;

BEGIN
  { get source filename }
  IF (ParamCount > 0) THEN
    sourceFile := ParamStr(1)
  ELSE
    BEGIN
      { get the filename from the user }
      Write('Enter source filename: ');
```

```
      Readln(sourceFile);
    END;
  { get target filename }
  IF (ParamCount > 1) THEN
    targetFile := ParamStr(2)
  ELSE
    BEGIN
      { get the filename from the user }
      Write('Enter target filename: ');
      Readln(targetfile);
    END;

  { assign the input filename to the file pointer }
  Assign(inputFile, sourceFile);

  { rename the file }
  { disable I/O checking }
  {$I-}
  Rename(inputFile, targetFile);
  { enable I/O checking }
  {$I+}

  { test Rename's success }
  IF (IOResult <> 0) THEN
    Writeln('Error renaming ', sourceFile,
      ' to ', targetFile)
  ELSE
    Writeln(sourceFile, ' renamed to ',
      targetFile);
END.
```

Related routines: Assign, Erase, IOResult

Reset   System

Opens an existing file for input operations.

Syntax
PROCEDURE Reset(VAR *filePointer*: *<file type>*
  [; *blockSize*: Word]);

Arguments

filePointer is a file pointer previously assigned to the filename by Assign.

blockSize specifies the block size for file transfers to untyped files. The default block size is 128 bytes.

Notes

The Reset procedure opens a text file for read-only operations. For typed and untyped files, Reset opens the file for read and write operations.

Many programs use a block size that is a multiple of 512 to improve file performance.

If Reset cannot open the specified file, an I/O error occurs. You can trap this error by disabling I/O checking with the {$I-} compiler directive, resetting the file, enabling I/O checking with {$I+}, and then testing the IOResult function.

Example
See Append.

Related routines: Append, Assign, Close, Eof, IOResult, Rewrite

Rewrite   System

Creates a new file or overwrites an existing file and prepares it for output operations.

Syntax
PROCEDURE Rewrite(VAR *filePointer*: <file type>
   [; *blockSize*: Word]);

Arguments
filePointer is a file pointer previously assigned to the filename by Assign.

blockSize specifies the block size for file transfers to untyped files. The default block size is 128 bytes.

Notes

If Rewrite opens an existing file, any data in the file will be lost.

The Rewrite procedure opens a text file for output operations. For typed and untyped files, Rewrite opens the file for read and write operations.

Many programs use a block size that is a multiple of 512 to improve file performance.

If Rewrite cannot open the specified file, an I/O error occurs. You can trap this error by disabling I/O checking with the {$I–} compiler directive, resetting the file, enabling I/O checking with {$I+}, and then testing the IOResult function.

Example
See AssignCrt.

Related routines: Append, Assign, Close, Eof, IOResult, Reset

RmDir   System

Removes the specified directory from disk.

Syntax
PROCEDURE RmDir(*pathname*: <*string type*>);

Arguments
pathname is a character string containing the name of the subdirectory to be deleted.

Notes
The RmDir procedure behaves as the DOS RMDIR command does. You cannot delete the current directory or any directory containing files.

If RmDir cannot remove the specified directory, an I/O error occurs. You can trap this error by disabling I/O checking with {$I–}, calling RmDir, enabling I/O checking with {$I+} and then testing IOResult. If RmDir was successful, IOResult returns 0; otherwise, RmDir returns an error status value.

Example

```
PROGRAM RemoveDirectory;

VAR
  directory: STRING;  { directory to remove }

BEGIN
  Write('Enter name of directory to remove: ');
  Readln(directory);

  {$I-} { disable I/O checking }
  RmDir(directory);
  {$I+} { enable I/O checking }

  IF (IOResult <> 0) THEN
    Writeln('Error removing ', directory)
  ELSE
    Writeln('Directory ', directory, ' removed');
END.
```

Related routines: ChDir, GetDir, IOResult, MkDir

Round   System

Rounds a floating-point value to the nearest whole number.

Syntax
PROCEDURE Round(*value*: <*real type*>): LongInt;

Arguments
value is the floating-point value that Round rounds to the nearest whole number.

Notes
If the return value exceeds the range of a LongInt value, a run-time error occurs.

Example
```
PROGRAM RoundAndTrunc;
VAR
  a, b: Real;

BEGIN
  a := 99.995;
  b := 100.995;

  Writeln('Rounding   ', a:6:3, Round(a):6);
  Writeln('Truncating ', a:6:3, Trunc(a):6);
  Writeln('Rounding   ', b:6:3, Round(b):5);
  Writeln('Truncating ', b:6:3, Trunc(b):5);
END.
```

Related routines: Frac, Int, Trunc

RunError   System

Generates the specified run-time error, thus ending program execution.

Syntax
PROCEDURE RunError[(*errorCode*: Word)];

Arguments
errorCode is the status code that corresponds to the desired run-time error. If you omit the argument, RunError uses the value 0.

Notes
If an error message corresponds to the specified status code, QuickPascal displays the error message before the program ends.

The program also returns this error code to the operating system as its exit status value. DOS batch files can test this status value using the DOS command IF ERRORLEVEL.

Example

```
PROGRAM GenerateRunError;

BEGIN
  { generate program-specific run-time error }
  RunError(33);
END.
```

Related routines: DosExitCode, Exec, Exit, Halt

_ScrollTextWindow — MSGraph

Scrolls text vertically in the current text window.

Syntax
PROCEDURE _ScrollTextWindow(*numLines*: Integer);

Arguments
numLines is the number of lines to scroll up or down. A positive number scrolls lines up. A negative number scrolls lines down.

Notes
The MSGraph unit defines the following constants for single-line scrolling:

Constant	Meaning
_GScrollUp	Scroll text up one line.
_GScrollDown	Scroll text down one line.

Upon completion of the _ScrollTextWindow procedure, the _GrStatus function returns the following error status value:

Value	Meaning
_GrNoOutput	Text not scrolled

Related routines: _GrStatus, _OutText, _SetTextWindow

Seek

System

Moves the current file position to a specific location.

Syntax
PROCEDURE Seek(VAR *filePointer*: <typed or untyped file>; *index*: LongInt);

Arguments
filePointer refers to an open typed or untyped file.

index is the desired file position.

Notes
The file pointer cannot refer to a text file.

File index values begin at zero and increase by whole components or blocks.

Example
See FilePos.

Related routines: Eof, FilePos, IOResult

SeekEof

System

Tests whether a file pointer is at the end of a file, ignoring blanks, tabs, and end-of-line characters.

Syntax
FUNCTION SeekEof[(VAR *filePointer*: Text)]: Boolean;

Arguments
filePointer is an optional pointer to a text file.

Notes
The SeekEof function differs from Eof in that it ignores spaces, tabs, and end-of-line characters in searching for the end of a file.

If SeekEof encounters the end of the file, it returns true; otherwise, it returns false.

Related routines: Eof, SeekEoln

SeekEoln   System

Tests whether a file pointer is at the end of a line, ignoring blanks and tabs.

Syntax
FUNCTION SeekEoln[(VAR *filePointer*: Text)]: Boolean;

Arguments
filePointer is an optional pointer to a text file.

Notes
The SeekEoln function differs from the Eoln function in that it ignores blanks and tabs in searching for the end of the line.

If SeekEoln encounters an end-of-line character or the end of the file, it returns true; otherwise, it returns false.

Related routines: Eoln, SeekEof

Seg   System

Returns the segment address for a variable, function, or procedure.

Syntax
FUNCTION Seg(*identifier*: <*variable, function, or procedure*>): Word;

Arguments
identifier is the variable, function, or procedure for which Seg returns the segment address.

Notes

The IBM PC and PC-compatibles access memory locations using an address composed of a 16-bit segment and a 16-bit offset. The Seg function returns an identifier's segment address.

Example
See Ofs.

Related routines: Addr, CSeg, DSeg, Ofs, SPtr, SSeg

_SelectPalette
MSGraph

Selects the active palette.

Syntax
FUNCTION _SelectPalette(*paletteNumber*: Integer): Integer;

Arguments
paletteNumber is the desired palette (0 through 3).

Notes
The _MRes4Color video mode supports four different palettes.

Palette Number	Color 0	Color 1	Color 2	Color 3
0	Background	Green	Red	Brown
1	Background	Cyan	Magenta	White
2	Background	Light green	Light red	Yellow
3	Background	Light cyan	Light magenta	Bright white

The _SelectPalette function returns the previous palette number when it completes execution.

Upon completion of the _SelectPalette function, the _GrStatus function returns the following error status values.

Status	Meaning
_GrInvalidParameter	Invalid palette number
_GrNotInProperMode	Invalid video display mode

After your program selects a new palette, objects already present on the screen change colors accordingly.

Example

```pascal
PROGRAM ShowPalettes;

USES
  MSGraph,  { contains graphics routines }
  CRT;      { contains KeyPressed and ReadKey }

VAR
  status: Integer;
  paletteCount: Integer;
  oldPalette: Integer;
  buffer: Char;

BEGIN
  { set the video mode to 320 by 200 graphics }
  status := _SetVideoMode(_MRes4Color);

  _SetColor(1);
  _Rectangle(_GFillInterior, 55, 50, 110, 150);
  _SetColor(2);
  _Rectangle(_GFillInterior, 145, 50, 200, 150);
  _SetColor(3);
  _Rectangle(_GFillInterior, 235, 50, 290, 150);

  FOR paletteCount := 0 TO 3 DO
    BEGIN
      oldPalette := _SelectPalette (paletteCount);
      buffer := ReadKey;
    END;

  _SetTextPosition(23, 8);
  _OutText('Press any key to continue');

  WHILE (NOT KeyPressed) DO
    ;

  { restore the original video mode }
  status := _SetVideoMode(_DefaultMode);
END.
```

Related routines: _GetBkColor, _RemapAllPalette, _RemapPalette, _SetBkColor, _SetColor

_SetActivePage — MSGraph

Selects the active display page.

Syntax
PROCEDURE _SetActivePage(*pageNumber*: Integer);

Arguments
pageNumber is the page number of the desired display page.

Notes
The active video page is the display page to which the _OutText function writes text or the graphics functions draw images. The visual page is the page that appears on your screen display. When you write output to an active page and then select that page as the visual page, the output appears instantly on your screen.

The _GetVideoConfig procedure returns the number of available display pages.

Upon completion of the _SetActivePage procedure, the _GrStatus function returns the following error status value:

Status	Meaning
_GrInvalidParameter	Invalid page number in call to _SetActivePage

Related routines: _GetActivePage, _GetVideoConfig, _GetVisualPage, _GrStatus, _SetVisualPage

_SetBkColor — MSGraph

Selects the current background color.

Syntax

PROCEDURE _SetBkColor(*backgroundColor*: LongInt);

Arguments

backgroundColor is the desired background color.

Notes

In text mode the color value is normally a color index. In graphics mode the color value is a constant defined in the MSGraph unit.

In text mode, _SetBkColor does not change the current background color; it changes the background for subsequent output. In graphics mode, _SetBkColor changes the background color immediately.

Upon completion of the _SetBkColor procedure, the _GrStatus function returns the following status values:

Status	Meaning
_GrInvalidParameter	Invalid color value in call to _SetBkColor
_GrParameterAltered	Parameter altered to match range

Example

```
PROGRAM SetBackGroundColor;

USES
  MSGraph,  { contains graphics routines }
  Crt;      { contains the KeyPressed function }

VAR
  status: Integer;

BEGIN
  { set the video mode to 320 by 200 graphics }
  status := _SetVideoMode(_MRes4Color);

  { draw the filled rectangle }
  _Rectangle(_GFillInterior, 55, 50, 255, 150);

  _SetBkColor(_Blue);

  _SetTextPosition(23, 8);
  _OutText('Press any key to continue');
```

```
  WHILE (NOT KeyPressed) DO
    ;

  { restore the original video mode }
  status := _SetVideoMode(_DefaultMode);
END.
```

Related routines: _GetBkColor, _GrStatus, _RemapAllPalette, _RemapPalette, _SelectPalette, _SetColor, _SetTextColor

SetCBreak   Dos

Sets the state of DOS Ctrl+Break checking.

Syntax
PROCEDURE SetCBreak(*state*: Boolean);

Arguments
state specifies the state of extended Ctrl+Break checking. If *state* is true, DOS performs extended Ctrl+Break checking.

Notes
By default, DOS checks for a user-entered Ctrl+Break only after I/O to or from a communication port, the console, or the printer. When extended Ctrl+Break testing is enabled, DOS tests for a user-entered Ctrl+Break after each system service.

Example
```
PROGRAM SetCtrlBreak;

USES
  Dos;

VAR
  state: Boolean;
```

(continued)

continued

```
BEGIN
  { enable extended Ctrl+Break checking }
  state := True;
  SetCBreak(state);

  { statements }

  { DOS restores the previous setting when the
    program ends }
END.
```

Related routines: GetCBreak, GetVerify, SetVerify

_SetClipRgn   MSGraph

Defines the graphics clipping region.

Syntax
PROCEDURE _SetClipRgn(*upperLeftx*, *upperLefty*, *lowerRightx*, *lowerRighty*: Integer);

Arguments
upperLeftx and *upperLefty* are the *x* and *y* coordinates of the clipping region's upper left corner.

lowerRightx and *lowerRighty* are the *x* and *y* coordinates of the clipping region's lower right corner.

Notes
The clipping region defines the screen region within which graphics can be drawn. It does not change the viewport origin.

Upon completion of the _SetClipRgn procedure, the _GrStatus function returns the following exit status values:

Status	Meaning
_GrNotInProperMode	Invalid video display mode
_GrParameterAltered	One or more parameters altered to stay within range

Example

```
PROGRAM ClippingRegion;

USES
  MSGraph,  { contains graphics routines }
  Crt;      { contains the KeyPressed function }

VAR
  status: Integer;

BEGIN
  { set the video mode to 320 by 200 graphics }
  status := _SetVideoMode(_MRes4Color);
  _SetClipRgn(0, 0, 319, 100);
  _Rectangle(_GFillInterior,
    100, 50, 180, 150); { part clipped }
  _Ellipse(_GBorder, 200, 50, 250, 150);
  _Pie(_GFillInterior, 10, 50, 55, 125, 1, 1,
    200, 130);
  _Ellipse(_GFillInterior, 10, 10, 40, 40);

  _SetTextPosition(23, 8);
  _OutText('Press any key to continue');

  WHILE (NOT KeyPressed) DO
    ;

  { restore the original video mode }
  status := _SetVideoMode(_DefaultMode);
END.
```

Related routines: _GrStatus, _SetViewOrg, _SetViewport

_SetColor   MSGraph

Sets the current color for graphics output.

Syntax
PROCEDURE _SetColor(*colorIndex*: Integer);

Arguments

colorIndex is the palette index of the desired color.

Notes

By default, the graphics routines use the color that corresponds to the highest palette index.

The following routines use the current graphics color: _Arc, _Ellipse, _FloodFill, _LineTo, _OutGText, _Pie, _Rectangle, and _SetPixel.

Upon completion of the _SetColor procedure, the _GrStatus function returns the following error status values:

Status	Meaning
_GrNotInProperMode	Invalid video display mode
_GrParameterAltered	Parameter altered to match range

Example

See _SelectPalette.

Related routines: _GetColor, _GrStatus, _RemapAllPalette, _RemapPalette

SetDate   Dos

Changes the current system date.

Syntax

PROCEDURE SetDate(*year*, *month*, *day*: Word);

Arguments

year is the desired year in the range 1980 through 2009.

month is the desired month in the range 1 through 12.

day is the desired day in the range 1 through 31.

Notes

The SetDate procedure changes the DOS system date in the same way as the DOS DATE command does.

If any of the date parameters is invalid, the system date is not changed.

Example

```
PROGRAM Christmas;

USES
  Dos;    { contains SetDate }

BEGIN
  SetDate(1990, 12, 25);
END.
```

Related routines: GetDate, GetTime, SetTime

SetFAttr   Dos

Changes a file's attributes.

Syntax
PROCEDURE SetFAttr(VAR *filePointer*: <*file type*>;
  attributeValue: Word);

Arguments
filePointer is a pointer to a file that has been assigned a filename but is not open.

attributeValue is a word value containing the desired file attributes.

Notes
The Dos unit defines the following file attributes:

Attribute	Value
ReadOnly	$01
Hidden	$02
SysFile	$04
VolumeID	$08
Directory	$10
Archive	$20

To assign multiple attributes, use the plus operator as shown here:

```
SetFAttr(filePointer, ReadOnly + Archive);
```

When the SetFAttr procedure completes execution, your program can test the DosError global variable for the following status values:

Value	Meaning
0	Successful
3	Path not found
5	Access denied

Related routines: Assign, FindFirst, FindNext, GetFAttr, GetFTime, SetFTime

_SetFillMask
MSGraph

Defines the fill pattern used for graphics fill operations.

Syntax
PROCEDURE _SetFillMask(*newMask*: _FillMask);

Arguments
newMask is an 8-by-8-bit mask in which each bit in the mask corresponds to a pixel position in the fill mask. If a bit in the fill mask is 1, the pixel is on. If a bit is 0, the pixel is off.

Notes
By default, each bit in the fill mask is 1, which results in a solid fill pattern. The following routines fill objects using the current fill mask: _Ellipse, _FloodFill, _Pie, and _Rectangle.

When the _SetFillMask procedure completes execution, the _GrStatus function returns the following status value:

Status	Meaning
_GrNotInProperMode	Invalid video display mode

Example
See _GetFillMask.

Related routines: _Ellipse, _FloodFill, _GetFillMask, _GrStatus, _Pie, _Rectangle

_SetFont   MSGraph

Searches the list of registered fonts for a font matching the specified characteristics.

Syntax
FUNCTION _SetFont(*fontCharacteristics*: CSTRING): Integer;

Arguments
fontCharacteristics is a character string that contains one or more of the following characteristics:

Characteristic	Specifies
t''FontName''	Typeface
h*Number*	Font pixel height
w*Number*	Font pixel width
f	Fixed-space font
p	Proportionally spaced font
v	Vector font
r	Raster (bit-mapped) font
b	Best-fit font
n*number*	Font index number

Notes
The f and p and the v and r font characteristics are mutually exclusive.

If successful, _SetFont returns the font number. If an error occurs, _SetFont returns a negative value.

The following typeface names are valid for the t characteristic.

Typeface Name	Description
Courier	Fixed-width raster font with serifs
Helv	Proportional raster font without serifs
Tms Rmn	Proportional raster font with serifs
Script	Proportional vector font with slanted characters
Modern	Proportional vector font without serifs
Roman	Proportional vector font with serifs

To select a font, the _SetFont function uses the following precedence:

1. Pixel height
2. Typeface
3. Pixel width
4. Fixed or proportional font

If the specified font size does not exist, _SetFont can scale vector-based fonts to a close approximation.

The only output routine that supports fonts is _OutGText.

If the request for a font fails (a match was not found) and the b (best-fit) option is not specified, _SetFont returns an error value.

Upon completion of the _SetFont function, the _GrStatus function returns the following error status values:

Status	Meaning
_GrError	General graphics error
_GrFontFileNotFound	No matching font
_GrInsufficientMemory	Not enough memory to complete operation
_GrParameterAltered	One or more parameters altered to match range

Example

```
PROGRAM CenterStrings;

USES
  MSGraph,   { contains graphics routines }
  Crt;       { contains the ReadKey function }
```

```pascal
VAR
  status: Integer;
  numFonts: Integer;
  buffer: Char;
  fontInfo: _FontInfo;

BEGIN
  { set the video mode to 320 by 200 graphics }
  status := _SetVideoMode(_MRes4Color);

  { register the available fonts }
  numFonts := _RegisterFonts('*.FON');

  IF (numFonts < 1) THEN
    _OutText('No fonts loaded')
  ELSE
    BEGIN
      _SetTextPosition(2, 8);
      _OutText('Press any key to continue');

      status := _SetFont('t''Script''h72w26b');
      _MoveTo((320 -
        _GetGTextExtent('Microsoft')) DIV 2,
        30);
      _OutGText('Microsoft');
      _MoveTo ((320 -
        _GetGTextExtent('QuickPascal')) DIV 2,
        100);
      _OutGText('QuickPascal');

      buffer := ReadKey;

      { unregister the fonts }
      _UnRegisterFonts;
    END;

  { restore the original video mode }
  status := _SetVideoMode(_DefaultMode);
END.
```

Related routines: _GetFontInfo, _GetGTextExtent, _GrStatus, _OutGText, _RegisterFonts, _SetGTextVector, _UnRegisterFonts

SetFTime — Dos

Sets a file's date and time stamp.

Syntax
PROCEDURE SetFTime(VAR *filePointer*: <file type>;
  dateTimeStamp: LongInt);

Arguments
filePointer is a pointer to an open file.

dateTimeStamp is the desired date and time stamp in a packed format.

Notes
The SetFTime procedure changes the date and time stamp that appears in the directory listing of a file.

If the file is open for write operations and has been written to, DOS will update the file's date and time stamp as soon as the file is closed.

When the SetFTime procedure completes execution, your program can test the DosError global variable for the following status values:

Status	Meaning
0	Successful
6	Invalid file handle

Related routines: FindFirst, FindNext, GetFTime, PackTime, UnpackTime

_SetGTextVector — MSGraph

Changes the orientation of font text displayed by _OutGText.

Syntax
PROCEDURE _SetGTextVector(*x, y*: Integer);

Arguments
x and *y* define the vector specifying the font orientation as follows:

x	y	Orientation
1	0	Horizontal text
0	1	90 degrees counterclockwise
−1	0	180 degrees
0	−1	270 degrees counterclockwise

Notes
The _OutGText procedure lets your program display text in graphics mode. The _SetGTextVector procedure lets your program change the text orientation.

Upon completion of the _SetGTextVector procedure, the _GrStatus function returns the following error status value:

Status	Meaning
_GrParameterAltered	One or both parameters altered to match allowable values

Related routines: _GetGTextExtent, _GetGTextVector, _GrStatus, _OutGText, _SetFont

SetIntVec Dos

Specifies an address for an interrupt handler.

Syntax
PROCEDURE SetIntVec(*interruptNumber*: Byte;
    handlerAddress: Pointer);

Arguments
interruptNumber is the number of an interrupt in the range 0 through 255.

handlerAddress is a 32-bit pointer to the new interrupt handler.

Notes
The @ operator and the Addr function return the address of a function or procedure.

If your program changes an interrupt handler during processing, the program should first save the original handler address, using GetIntVec, so that it can restore the original setting before ending.

Related routines: Addr, Intr, GetIntVec, SwapVectors

_SetLineStyle — MSGraph

Defines the line style used to draw lines in graphics mode.

Syntax
PROCEDURE _SetLineStyle(*lineStyle*: Word);

Arguments
lineStyle is a 16-bit value that corresponds to 16 pixels in a line. If a bit in the line style is 1, the corresponding pixel is on. If a bit in the line style is 0, the pixel is off.

Notes
The default line style is $FFFF, or all bits equal to one, a solid line.

Example
```
PROGRAM LineStyles;

USES
  MSGraph,  { contains graphics routines }
  Crt;      { contains the KeyPressed function }

VAR
  status: Integer;
```

```
BEGIN
  { set the video mode to 320 by 200 graphics }
  status := _SetVideoMode(_MRes4Color);

  _SetTextPosition(3, 2);
  _OutText('$FFFF');
  _MoveTo(100, 20);
  _LineTo(250, 20);

  _SetTextPosition(6, 2);
  _OutText('$F0F0');
  _SetLineStyle($F0F0);
  _MoveTo(100, 43);
  _LineTo(250, 43);

  _SetTextPosition(23, 8);
  _OutText('Press any key to continue');

  WHILE (NOT KeyPressed) DO
    ;

  { restore the original video mode }
  status := _SetVideoMode(_DefaultMode);
END.
```

Related routines: _GetLineStyle, _LineTo, _Pie, _Rectangle

_SetPixel   MSGraph

Turns on the pixel at the specified viewport coordinates, using the current color.

Syntax
PROCEDURE _SetPixel(*x, y*: Integer);

Arguments
x and *y* are the logical (viewport) coordinates of the desired pixel.

Notes

Upon completion of the _SetPixel procedure, the _GrStatus function returns the following error status values:

Status	Meaning
_GrNoOutput	Pixel not set
_GrNotInProperMode	Invalid video display mode

Example

```
PROGRAM SetPixels;

USES
  MSGraph,  { contains graphics routines }
  Crt;      { contains the KeyPressed function }

VAR
  status: Integer;
  x: Integer;

BEGIN
  { set the video mode to 320 by 200 graphics }
  status := _SetVideoMode(_MRes4Color);

  FOR x := 70 TO 250 DO
    _SetPixel(x, 100);

  _SetTextPosition(23, 8);
  _OutText('Press any key to continue');

  WHILE (NOT KeyPressed) DO
    ;

  { restore the original video mode }
  status := _SetVideoMode(_DefaultMode);
END.
```

Related routines: _GetPixel, _GrStatus, _SetColor

_SetPixel_w   MSGraph

Turns on the pixel at the specified window coordinates, using the current color.

Syntax
PROCEDURE _SetPixel_w(*realx*, *realy*: Double);

Arguments
realx and *realy* are the *x* and *y* window (floating-point) coordinates of the desired pixel.

Notes
Upon completion of the _SetPixel_w procedure, the _GrStatus function returns the following error status values:

Status	Meaning
_GrNoOutput	Pixel not set
_GrNotInProperMode	Invalid video display mode

Related routines: _GetPixel_w, _GrStatus, _SetColor

SetTextBuf   System

Defines the I/O buffer and, optionally, the buffer size for text-file operations.

Syntax
PROCEDURE SetTextBuf(VAR *filePointer*: Text;
  VAR buffer: <*any type*> [; *bufferSize*: Word]);

Arguments
filePointer is a pointer to a text file.

buffer is a memory buffer to be used for I/O operations to the file.

bufferSize is an optional buffer size. The default size is 128 bytes.

Notes
For text files that perform a large number of I/O operations, it is often helpful to specify a large buffer to improve performance. Buffer sizes should normally be integer multiples of 512.

Do not call SetTextBuf for open files that your program has read from or written data to. Doing so might result in loss of data.

Do not use a local variable for a text buffer if the file will remain open after the procedure completes execution.

Example
See Append.

Related routines: Append, Assign, AssignCrt, Close, Read, Readln, Reset, Rewrite, SizeOf, Write, Writeln

_SetTextColor

MSGraph

Selects the current color for text output.

Syntax
PROCEDURE _SetTextColor(*colorIndex*: Integer);

Arguments
colorIndex is the desired color index value from 0 through 31 that selects one of the following colors:

Color Index	Color	Color Index	Color
0	Black	8	Dark gray
1	Blue	9	Light blue
2	Green	10	Light green
3	Cyan	11	Light cyan
4	Red	12	Light red
5	Magenta	13	Light magenta
6	Brown	14	Yellow
7	White	15	Bright white

Notes
Adding 16 to a color index produces the same color but with the blink attribute enabled.

The selected color affects output from _OutMem and _OutText only.

Upon completion of the _SetTextColor procedure, the _GrStatus function returns the following error status value:

Status	Meaning
_GrParameterAltered	Color index altered to match range

Example

```
PROGRAM TextColors;

USES
  MSGraph;   { contains _SetTextColor and _OutText }

CONST
  { carriage return + linefeed }
  CrLf: STRING = #13 + #10;

VAR
  color: Integer;
  buffer: STRING;

BEGIN
  FOR color := 0 TO 15 DO
    BEGIN
      _SetTextColor(color);
      Str(color, buffer);
      _OutText('The current color is ' +
        buffer + CrLf);
    END;
END.
```

Related routines: _GetTextColor, _GrStatus, _OutMem, _OutText

_SetTextCursor — MSGraph

Defines the text cursor size.

Syntax
PROCEDURE _SetTextCursor(*cursorShape*: Word);

Arguments

cursorShape is the value the BIOS video routines use to set the cursor shape. The high-order byte determines the cursor's beginning scan line. The low-order byte determines the cursor's ending scan line.

Notes

The following table provides values for some common cursor sizes:

Value	Cursor Shape
$0707	Underscore cursor
$0007	Full block cursor
$0607	Double-underscore cursor
$2000	No cursor

Upon completion of the _SetTextCursor procedure, the _GrStatus function returns the following error status value:

Status	Meaning
_GrNotInProperMode	Invalid video display mode

Example

```
PROGRAM SetCursor;

USES
  MSGraph;

BEGIN
  _SetTextCursor($0007);
END.
```

Related routines: _GetTextCursor, _GrStatus

_SetTextPosition   MSGraph

Sets the text cursor position to the specified row and column.

Syntax

PROCEDURE _SetTextPosition(*row*, *column*: Integer);

Arguments

row and *column* are the desired cursor positions within the text window. The upper left window position is row 1, column 1.

Notes

_SetTextPosition works in text mode and graphics mode. The procedure sets the cursor for output from _OutMem, _OutText, Write, and Writeln.

Upon completion of the _SetTextPosition procedure, the _GrStatus function returns the following status value:

Status	Meaning
_GrParameterAltered	One or both parameters altered to match range

Example

See _Ellipse_w.

Related routines: _GetTextPosition, _OutMem, _OutText, _SetTextWindow

_SetTextRows   MSGraph

Defines the number of text rows for the current EGA or VGA video mode.

Syntax

FUNCTION _SetTextRows(*numRows*: Integer): Integer;

Arguments

numRows is the number of text rows desired. The default setting is 25.

Notes

The _SetTextRows function is valid for EGA and VGA adapters only. EGA adapters support 25 and 43 lines. VGA adapters support 25, 43, and 50 lines in most modes and 30 and 60 lines in _VRes16Color and _VRes2Color.

If successful, _SetTextRows returns the number of rows selected. If an error occurs, it returns 0.

Upon completion of the _SetTextRows function, the _GrStatus function returns the following status values:

Status	Meaning
_GrInvalidParameter	Invalid number of rows for current video mode
_GrParameterAltered	Parameter altered to match allowable values

Related routines: _GrStatus, _OutText, _SetTextWindow, _SetVideoMode, _SetVideoModeRows

_SetTextWindow   MSGraph

Defines the rows and columns in the current text window.

Syntax
PROCEDURE _SetTextWindow(*topRow*, *leftColumn*, *bottomRow*, *rightColumn*: Integer);

Arguments
topRow is the number of the current text window's top row.

leftColumn is the number of the current text window's leftmost column.

bottomRow is the number of the current text window's bottom row.

rightColumn is the number of the current text window's rightmost column.

Notes
The text window defines the screen area to which all text written by _OutText and _OutMem is restricted. Although a program can divide the screen into several different output areas, only one text window is active at any given time.

The text window does not affect output from the font-based _OutGText procedure.

Upon completion of the _SetTextWindow procedure, the _GrStatus function returns the following status value:

Status	Meaning
_GrParameterAltered	One or more parameters altered to match range

Related routines: _ClearScreen, _GetTextPosition, _GrStatus, _OutMem, _OutText, _ScrollTextWindow, _SetTextPosition, _WrapOn

SetTime   Dos

Sets the current system time.

Syntax
PROCEDURE SetTime(*hours, minutes, seconds, hundredths*: Word);

Arguments
hours is the current hour from 0 through 23 (0 is midnight, 12 is noon).

minutes is the current minute from 0 through 59.

seconds is the current second from 0 through 59.

hundredths is the current hundredth of a second from 0 through 99.

Notes
The SetTime procedure changes the system time in the same manner as the DOS TIME command does.

If any of the time parameters is invalid, SetTime does not change the system time.

Example

```
PROGRAM SetSystemTime;

USES
  Dos;  { contains SetTime procedure }

BEGIN
  { set time to midnight }
  SetTime(0, 0, 0, 0);
END.
```

Related routines: GetDate, GetTime, SetDate

SetVerify — Dos

Sets the disk verification state.

Syntax
PROCEDURE SetVerify(*verifyState*: Boolean);

Arguments
verifyState is a Boolean variable that, when true, directs DOS to enable disk verification. When *verifyState* is false, DOS disables disk verification.

Notes
The DOS VERIFY command enables and disables disk verification on a systemwide basis.

Example

```
PROGRAM SetDiskVerification;

USES
  Dos;

BEGIN
  { disable disk verification
    for better performance }
  SetVerify(False);

  { statements }
END.
```

Related routines: GetCBreak, GetVerify, SetCBreak

_SetVideoMode — MSGraph

Selects the current video mode.

Syntax
FUNCTION _SetVideoMode(*videoMode*: Integer): Integer;

Arguments
videoMode is the desired video mode.

Notes
The MSGraph unit defines constants for the various video modes. The following table describes each:

Mode	Meaning
_MaxResMode	Mode with highest possible resolution
_MaxColorMode	Mode with most available colors
_DefaultMode	Video mode when program began
_TextBW40	40-column 16-gray-shade text
_TextC40	40-column 16-color text
_TextBW80	80-column 16-gray-shade text
_TextC80	80-column 16-color text
_MRes4Color	320 × 200 4-color graphics
_MResNoColor	320 × 200 4-gray-shade graphics
_HResBW	640 × 200 black-and-white graphics
_TextMono	80-column monochrome text
_HercMono	720 × 348 black-and-white Hercules graphics
_MRes16Color	320 × 200 16-color graphics
_HRes16Color	640 × 200 16-color graphics
_EResNoColor	640 × 350 black-and-white graphics
_ERes2Color	640 × 350 4- or 16-color graphics
_VRes2Color	640 × 480 black-and-white graphics
_VRes16Color	640 × 480 16-color graphics
_MRes256Color	320 × 200 256-color graphics
_OResColor	640 × 400 Olivetti graphics

Upon completion, the _SetVideoMode function returns the previous video mode and the _GrStatus function returns the following error status values:

Status	Meaning
_GrError	General graphics error
_GrInvalidParameter	Invalid video mode value in call
_GrModeNotSupported	Video mode not supported by adapter

Example
See _Ellipse.

Related routines: _GetVideoConfig, _GrStatus, _SetTextRows, _SetVideoModeRows

_SetVideoModeRows — MSGraph

Sets the video mode and number of text rows in one operation.

Syntax
FUNCTION _SetVideoModeRows(*videoMode*, *numRows*: Integer): Integer;

Arguments
videoMode is the desired video mode. See _SetVideoMode.

numRows is the desired number of text rows. See _SetTextRows.

Notes
If successful, _SetVideoModeRows returns the number of rows set. If unsuccessful, _SetVideoModeRows returns 0.

Upon completion of the _SetVideoModeRows function, the _GrStatus function returns the following values.

Status	Meaning
_GrError	General graphics error
_GrInvalidParameter	Invalid video display mode or number of rows
_GrModeNotSupported	Video mode not supported by adapter

Related routines: _GetVideoConfig, _GrStatus, _SetTextRows, _SetVideoMode

_SetViewOrg — MSGraph

Moves the viewport origin to the specified logical (viewport) coordinates.

Syntax
PROCEDURE _SetViewOrg(*physx*, *physy*: Integer;
    VAR *previousOrigin*: _XYCoord);

Arguments
physx and *physy* are the physical coordinates to which the viewport origin will be relocated.

previousOrigin is a record of type _XYCoord that contains the previous viewport origin.

Notes
Upon completion of the _SetViewOrg function, the _GrStatus function returns the following error status value:

Status	Meaning
_GrNotInProperMode	Invalid video display mode

Example
```
PROGRAM LogicalOrigin;

USES
  MSGraph,  { contains graphics routines }
  Crt;      { contains the KeyPressed function }
```

(continued)

continued

```
VAR
  status: Integer;
  oldOrigin: _XYCoord;

BEGIN
  { set the video mode to 320 by 200 graphics }
  status := _SetVideoMode(_MRes4Color);

  { draw rectangle at the default origin }
  _Rectangle(_GFillInterior, 10, 10, 30, 30);

  { move the logical origin and redraw rectangle }
  _SetViewOrg(50, 50, oldOrigin);
  _Rectangle(_GFillInterior, 10, 10, 30, 30);

  { move the logical origin and redraw rectangle }
  _SetViewOrg(100, 100, oldOrigin);
  _Rectangle(_GFillInterior, 10, 10, 30, 30);

  _SetTextPosition(23, 8);
  _OutText('Press any key to continue');

  WHILE (NOT KeyPressed) DO
    ;

  { restore the original video mode }
  status := _SetVideoMode(_DefaultMode);
END.
```

Related routines: _GetPhysCoord, _GetViewCoord, _GetWindowCoord, _GrStatus, _SetClipRgn, _SetViewport

_SetViewport   MSGraph

Defines the clipping region and viewport origin for graphics output.

Syntax
PROCEDURE _SetViewport(*upperLeftx*, *upperLefty*, *lowerRightx*, *lowerRighty*: Integer);

Arguments

upperLeftx and *upperLefty* are the *x* and *y* coordinates of the viewport's upper left corner.

lowerRightx and *lowerRighty* are the *x* and *y* coordinates of the viewport's lower right corner.

Notes

The _SetViewport procedure combines the capabilities of the _SetClipRgn and _SetViewOrg procedures.

Upon completion of the _SetViewport procedure, the _GrStatus function returns the following error status values:

Status	Meaning
_GrNotInProperMode	Invalid video display mode
_GrParameterAltered	One or more parameters altered to match range

Example

```
PROGRAM Viewport;

USES
  MSGraph,   { contains graphics routines }
  Crt;       { contains the KeyPressed function }

VAR
  status: Integer;

BEGIN
  { set the video mode to 320 by 200 graphics }
  status := _SetVideoMode(_MRes4Color);

  _SetWindow(False, 0.0, 0.0, 100.0, 100.0);
  _Rectangle_w(_GFillInterior,
    35.0, 35.0, 50.0, 50.0);
  _Ellipse_w(_GFillInterior,
    60.0, 35.0, 85.0, 50.0);

  _SetViewport(0, 0, 160, 100);
  _Rectangle_w(_GFillInterior,
    35.0, 35.0, 50.0, 50.0);
  _Ellipse_w(_GFillInterior,
    60.0, 35.0, 85.0, 50.0);
```

(continued)

continued

```
  _SetViewport(0, 0, 80, 50);
  _Rectangle_w(_GFillInterior,
    35.0, 35.0, 50.0, 50.0);
  _Ellipse_w(_GFillInterior,
    60.0, 35.0, 85.0, 50.0);

  _SetTextPosition(23, 8);
  _OutText('Press any key to continue');

  WHILE (NOT KeyPressed) DO
    ;

  { restore the original video mode }
  status := _SetVideoMode(_DefaultMode);
END.
```

Related routines: _ClearScreen, _GrStatus, _SetClipRgn, _SetViewOrg, _SetWindow

_SetVisualPage   MSGraph

Selects the current visual display page.

Syntax
PROCEDURE _SetVisualPage(*pageNumber*: Integer);

Arguments
pageNumber is the page number of the desired video page.

Notes
The visual page is the page that appears on your screen. When you write to an active page and then select that page as the visual page, the output appears instantly on your screen. The active video page is the display page to which the _OutText procedure writes text or the graphics functions draw images.

The _GetVideoConfig procedure returns the number of available display pages in the current graphics mode.

Upon completion of the _SetVisualPage procedure, the _GrStatus function returns the following error status value:

Status   **Meaning**
_GrInvalidParameter   Invalid page number in call

Related routines: _GetActivePage, _GetVideoConfig, _GetVisualPage, _GrStatus, _SetActivePage, _SetVideoMode

_SetWindow   MSGraph

Defines the window (floating-point) coordinates.

Syntax
PROCEDURE _SetWindow(*invertOrigin*: Boolean;
  upperLeftx, *upperLefty*, *lowerRightx*, *lowerRighty*:
  Double);

Arguments
invertOrigin is a Boolean flag that, when true, directs _SetWindow to invert the window, placing the origin at the lower left corner of the screen. When this flag is false, _SetWindow uses the default origin at the upper left corner.

upperLeftx and *upperLefty* are the floating-point window coordinates of the window's upper left corner.

lowerRightx and *lowerRighty* are the floating-point window coordinates of the window's lower right corner.

Notes
The QuickPascal graphics routines support physical, logical (viewport), and window coordinates. Window coordinates give your program the greatest flexibility because with them your program can describe an object using a scale that best fits the object. The graphics routines automatically map these coordinates to the correct pixel locations.

Window transformations performed by _SetWindow apply to the current viewport, not to the entire screen display.

Upon completion of the _SetWindow procedure, the _GrStatus function returns the following error status values:

Status	Meaning
_GrInvalidParameter	Invalid parameter in call to _SetWindow
_GrNotInProperMode	Invalid video display mode
_GrParameterAltered	One or more parameters altered to match range

Example
See _Ellipse_w.

Related routines: _GetWindowCoord, _GrStatus, _SetViewport

_SetWriteMode   MSGraph

Defines the logical line mode used in conjunction with the current line style.

Syntax
PROCEDURE _SetWriteMode(*lineMode*: Integer);

Arguments
lineMode is the desired logical line mode: _GPSET, _GAND, _GOR, _GXOR, or _GPRESET.

Notes
The logical write mode specifies how lines are drawn on your screen in cases in which pixels are currently on. The following line modes are supported.

Mode	Action
_GPSET	Causes the line to be drawn in the current color (default)
_GAND	Performs a logical AND of the pixels in each line position
_GOR	Performs a logical OR of the pixels in each line position
_GXOR	Performs an exclusive OR of the line pixels with the current screen pixels
_GPRESET	Draws the line inverting the current line style

The _GrStatus function returns the following status values for _SetWriteMode:

Status	Meaning
_GrNotInProperMode	Invalid video display mode
_GrInvalidParameter	Invalid line mode in call

Related routines: _GetWriteMode, _GrStatus, _LineTo, _PutImage, _Rectangle

Sin
System

Returns the sine of an angle expressed in radians.

Syntax
FUNCTION Sin(*angle*: <*real type*>): <*real type*>;

Arguments
angle is an angle expressed in radians.

Notes
The angle your program passes to Sin must be expressed in radians. To convert degrees to radians, use the following equation:

Radians = Degrees / $180.0 * \pi$;

Example

```
PROGRAM Sine;

BEGIN
  { use Alt+227 to create π }
  Writeln('Sine of π is ', Sin(Pi));
  Writeln('Sine of π/2 is ', Sin(Pi/2));
END.
```

Related routines: ArcTan, Cos, Pi

SizeOf   System

Returns the size, in bytes, of a variable or data type.

Syntax
FUNCTION SizeOf(*identifier*: <*any type*>): Word;

Arguments
identifier is the variable or type identifier for which SizeOf returns the size in bytes.

Notes
Before using the GetMem and New procedures to allocate memory dynamically, use SizeOf to determine the number of available bytes.

Example

```
PROGRAM Sizes;

BEGIN
  Writeln('Integer: ', SizeOf(Integer));
  Writeln('Byte: ', SizeOf(Byte));
  Writeln('Real: ', SizeOf(Real));

  Writeln('Double: ', SizeOf(Double));
END.
```

Related routines: FillChar, FreeMem, GetMem, MaxAvail, Move, New

Sound
Crt

Generates a tone from the computer's built-in speaker.

Syntax
PROCEDURE Sound(*frequency*: Word);

Arguments
frequency is the tone's frequency in hertz (cycles per second).

Notes
After it's turned on, the tone remains on until your program calls the NoSound procedure.

The Delay procedure lets your program temporarily suspend execution so that the tone can be heard.

Example
See Delay.

Related routines: Delay, KeyPressed, NoSound, ReadKey

SPtr
System

Returns the value of the stack pointer register.

Syntax
FUNCTION SPtr: Word;

Arguments
None.

Notes
The stack pointer register stores the 16-bit offset address of the top of the stack. The stack holds local variables and information for function and procedure calls.

Example
See CSeg.

Related routines: Addr, CSeg, DSeg, Ofs, Ptr, Seg, SSeg

Sqr
System

Returns the square of the specified value.

Syntax
FUNCTION Sqr(*value*: <Integer *or* Real>):
  <*same type as argument*>;

Arguments
value is the value for which Sqr returns the square.

Notes
A number's square is equivalent to the number multiplied by itself.

Example
```
PROGRAM SqrTest;

VAR
  a, b: Integer;

BEGIN
  a := 5;
  b := 3;

  Writeln('Sqr of', a:2, ' is', Sqr(a):3);
  Writeln('Sqr of', b:2, ' is', Sqr(b):3);
  Writeln('Sqr of', a:2, ' +', b:2, ' is',
    Sqr(a + b):3);

  Writeln('Sqr of', a:2, ' *', b:2, ' is',
    Sqr(a * b):4);
END.
```

Related routines: Abs, Sqrt

Sqrt

System

Returns the square root of the specified value.

Syntax
FUNCTION Sqrt(*value*: <Integer *or* Real>): Real;

Arguments
value is the value for which Sqrt returns the square root.

Notes
If the value passed to Sqrt is negative, a run-time error occurs.

Example
```
PROGRAM SquareRoot;

VAR
  value: Integer;
  result: Real;

BEGIN
  FOR value := 1 TO 100 DO
    BEGIN
      result := Sqrt(value);
      Writeln('Value', value:4,
        ' Square root '; result:7:4);
    END;
END.
```

Related routines: Abs, Sqr

SSeg

System

Returns the value of the stack segment register.

Syntax
FUNCTION SSeg: Word;

Arguments

None.

Notes

The stack segment register stores the 16-bit stack segment address. The stack holds local variables and information for function and procedure calls.

Example

See CSeg.

Related routines: Addr, CSeg, DSeg, Ofs, Ptr, Seg, SPtr

Str   System

Converts a number to its character-string representation.

Syntax

PROCEDURE Str(*number*[<*format*>]: <Integer *or* Real>;
    VAR *targetString*: <*string type*>);

Arguments

number is the numeric value Str represents as a character string.

targetString is the character-string variable to which Str assigns the number's character-string value.

Notes

The optional format specifies the width of and the number of decimal places in the resulting character string. The format is similar to that used by Write and Writeln. Str does not support hexadecimal output.

Example

See _SetTextColor.

Related routines: Concat, Copy, Delete, Insert, Length, Pos, Val, Write, Writeln

Succ

System

Returns an ordinal value's succeeding value.

Syntax
FUNCTION Succ(*ordinalValue*: <*ordinal type*>):
  <*same type as argument*>;

Arguments
ordinalValue is the ordinal value for which Succ returns the successor value.

Notes
Ordinal types include Boolean, Char, integer types, and subrange and enumerated types.

If you use Succ to return the ordinal following the last ordinal in a type, a range error occurs.

Example
See First.

Related routines: Dec, First, Inc, Last, Ord, Pred

Swap

System

Exchanges the high and low bytes of an integer or word value.

Syntax
FUNCTION Swap(*value*: <Integer *or* Word>):
  <*same type as argument*>;

Arguments
value is the integer or word value whose high and low bytes Swap exchanges.

Notes

Your program can pass any integer type to Swap. If your program uses Swap for a Byte or LongInt value, the return value might be confusing.

Related routines: Hi, Lo

SwapVectors   Dos

Exchanges interrupt vector addresses with their previously saved values.

Syntax
PROCEDURE SwapVectors;

Arguments
None.

Notes

The System unit defines 18 pointers named SaveInt*nn*, where *nn* is a specific interrupt number.

A program that modifies interrupt vectors and uses the Exec procedure should call SwapVectors to set interrupt vector addresses to their original contents before calling Exec. Doing so prevents the child process from using interrupts modified by the parent process. When Exec completes execution, the program should call SwapVectors a second time to restore the vector addresses used by the parent process.

Example
See DosExitCode.

Related routines: Exec, GetIntVec, Intr, MsDos, SetIntVec

TextBackground   Crt

Selects the background color for text output.

Syntax
PROCEDURE TextBackground(*backgroundColor*: Byte);

Arguments
backgroundColor is a byte value in the range 0 through 7 that specifies one of the following colors:

Value	Color	Value	Color
0	Black	4	Red
1	Blue	5	Magenta
2	Green	6	Brown
3	Cyan	7	White

Notes
If the color value specified exceeds 7, TextBackground uses only the three lowest bits, yielding a value in the range 0 through 7.

To change the entire screen's background color, call TextBackground followed immediately by ClrScr.

Example
```
PROGRAM BackgroundColors;

USES
  Crt;           { contains TextBackground }

VAR
  color: Integer;   { background color }

BEGIN
  FOR color := 0 TO 7 DO
    BEGIN
      TextBackground(color);
      ClrScr;
      Writeln('Current color: ', color);
      Delay(1000);
    END;
  TextBackground(0);    { restore dark background }
END.
```

Related routines: ClrScr, HighVideo, LowVideo, NormVideo, TextColor, TextMode, Window

TextColor

Crt

Selects the character foreground color for text output.

Syntax
PROCEDURE TextColor(*foregroundColor*: Byte);

Arguments
foregroundColor is a byte value that specifies one of the following colors:

Color Index	Color	Color Index	Color
0	Black	8	Dark gray
1	Blue	9	Light blue
2	Green	10	Light green
3	Cyan	11	Light cyan
4	Red	12	Light red
5	Magenta	13	Light magenta
6	Brown	14	Yellow
7	White	15	Bright white

Notes
The Crt unit defines the constant Blink, which, when added to the color value, produces a blinking color.

Example
```
PROGRAM TextColors;

USES
  Crt;            { contains TextColor procedure }

VAR
  color: Integer;
```

```
BEGIN
  FOR color := 0 TO 15 DO
    BEGIN
      TextColor(color);
      Writeln('Current color is ', color);
    END;
END.
```

Related routines: HighVideo, LowVideo, NormVideo, TextBackground, TextMode, Window

TextMode   Crt

Selects the specified text video-display mode.

Syntax
PROCEDURE TextMode(*textVideoMode*: Integer);

Arguments
textVideoMode is an integer value describing the desired text mode. The Crt unit defines several text-mode constants.

Notes
The Crt unit defines the following variables for use with TextMode:

Variable	Meaning
DirectVideo	Directs QuickPascal to perform memory-mapped video output.
CheckSnow	Directs QuickPascal to perform video-refresh synchronization to prevent "snow" on CGA screens.
LastMode	Stores the current text mode. If the program selects graphics mode, it can later easily select the previous text mode, using LastMode.
TextAttr	Sets the text attributes to those of the character at the current cursor position.

Related routines: HighVideo, LowVideo, NormVideo, TextBackground, TextColor, Window

Trunc
System

Truncates a floating-point value to a LongInt value.

Syntax
FUNCTION Trunc(*number*: <*integer or real type*>): LongInt;

Arguments
number is the value the Trunc function truncates.

Notes
Trunc discards the fractional portion of a floating-point number, returning a whole number. For a rounded value, use the Round function.

Example
See Round.

Related routines: Frac, Int, Round

Truncate
System

Truncates a file's contents at the current file position.

Syntax
PROCEDURE Truncate(VAR *filePtr*: <*typed or untyped file*>);

Arguments
filePtr is a pointer to an open file.

Notes
Do not use Truncate with text files.

All information between the file pointer and the end of the file is lost.

If the pointer does not point to an open file, an I/O error occurs.

Related routines: BlockRead, BlockWrite, Eof, FilePos, FileSize, IOResult, Reset, Rewrite, Seek

UnpackTime — Dos

Converts the date and time information normally stored in packed format in a LongInt value to a record of type DateTime that contains the individual date and time components.

Syntax
PROCEDURE UnpackTime(*packedDateTime*: LongInt;
    VAR *dateTimeRecord*: DateTime);

Arguments
packedDateTime is a LongInt value that contains the date and time in packed format.

dateTimeRecord is a record of type DateTime that contains the individual date and time components.

Notes
The compressed date and time are stored in a LongInt value, as shown in Figure 3.

Bit	31–26	25–22	21–17	16–12	11–6	5–0
Value	Year	Month	Day	Hour	Minute	Second
Range	1–99	1–12	1–31	0–23	0–59	0–59

Figure 3. *The packed time format.*

The Dos unit defines the DateTime record as follows:

```
DateTime = RECORD
  Year, Month, Day, Hour, Min, Sec: Word;
END;
```

Related routines: FindFirst, FindNext, GetFTime, PackTime, SetFTime

_UnRegisterFonts   MSGraph

Removes font information previously installed by _RegisterFonts, thus freeing memory.

Syntax
PROCEDURE _UnRegisterFonts;

Arguments
None.

Notes
_UnRegisterFonts removes all font header information and releases the memory allocated for the fonts.

Example
See _SetFont.

Related routines: _GetFontInfo, _GetGTextExtent, _OutGText, _RegisterFonts, _SetFont, _SetGTextVector

UpCase   System

Converts a character to uppercase.

Syntax
FUNCTION UpCase(*character*: Char): Char;

Arguments

character is the lowercase letter to be converted to uppercase.

Notes

If the specified character is not lowercase, UpCase returns the character unchanged.

Example

See Eoln.

Related routines: Chr, Ord

Val System

Converts a character string representation of a value to the value it represents.

Syntax

PROCEDURE Val(ASCIIVal: <string type>; VAR *value*: <integer or real type>; VAR *errorIndex*: Integer);

Arguments

ASCIIVal is the character string representation of the value.

value is the numeric result.

errorIndex is the character index of the first invalid character in the string. If the entire string was converted, *errorIndex* is 0.

Notes

A string containing an integer representation can contain a plus or a minus sign and decimal or hexadecimal digits.

A string containing a floating-point representation can contain a signed decimal number, the letter E, and a signed exponent, such as +48.732E−6.

The Val and Str procedures perform inverse tasks.

Example

```
PROGRAM StringToValue;

VAR
  userInput: STRING;
  strItemCost: STRING;
  cost: Real;
  errorIndex: Integer;

BEGIN
  userInput := 'Meat 9.95';

  { copy the item cost '9.95'
    by searching for the space }
  strItemCost := Copy(userInput,
    Pos(' ', userInput) + 1, Length(userInput));

  { convert '9.95' to floating point }
  Val(strItemCost, cost, errorIndex);

  Writeln('Ending cost: $', cost:4:2);
END.
```

Related routines: Concat, Copy, Delete, Insert, Length, Pos, Str

WhereX   Crt

Returns the current cursor column position.

Syntax
FUNCTION WhereX: Byte;

Arguments
None.

Notes
The GotoXY procedure lets your program set the cursor position.

Related routines: GotoXY, WhereY

WhereY — Crt

Returns the current cursor row position.

Syntax
FUNCTION WhereY: Byte;

Arguments
None.

Notes
The GotoXY procedure lets your program set the cursor position.

Related routines: GotoXY, WhereX

Window — Crt

Defines the screen area to which text output is restricted.

Syntax
PROCEDURE Window(*upperLeftx*, *upperLefty*, *lowerRightx*, *lowerRighty*: Byte);

Arguments
upperLeftx and *upperLefty* are the column and row coordinates of the window's upper left corner.

lowerRightx and *lowerRighty* are the column and row coordinates of the window's lower right corner.

Notes
Using text windows lets your program restrict output to specific screen regions. Output from the following procedures is limited to the current text window: ClrEol, ClrScr, DelLine, GotoXY, InsLine, Read, Readln, WhereX, WhereY, Write, and Writeln.

When text reaches the bottom window row, the window text scrolls up one line.

Example
See DelLine.

Related routines: ClrEol, ClrScr, DelLine, GotoXY, InsLine, Read, Readln, WhereX, WhereY, Write, Writeln

_WrapOn   MSGraph

Determines whether text is truncated or wraps to the next line when it goes beyond the rightmost window column.

Syntax
FUNCTION _WrapOn(*state*: Boolean): Boolean;

Arguments
state defines the text-wrapping state. When *state* is true (the default), the _OutText and _OutMem functions wrap text to the next line when it extends beyond the rightmost column. When *state* is false, text is truncated beyond the rightmost column.

Notes
_WrapOn does not affect Write, Writeln, or _OutGText.

Related routines: _OutMem, _OutText, _ScrollTextWindow, _SetTextWindow

Write   System

Writes text, variables, and constants to a file or the screen.

Syntax
PROCEDURE Write([VAR *filePointer*: <Text *or typed file*>;] *expression*: <*simple or component type*>; [...]);

Arguments

filePointer is an optional pointer to a text or typed file that is open for output.

expression is the text or numeric data that Write is to put into a file or onto the screen.

Notes

If the call to Write does not include a file pointer, output is written to the screen.

For character or Boolean expressions, the output format is *expression*[:*width*], where the optional *width* specifies the minimum number of characters in the output.

For numeric expressions, the output format is *expression* [:*width*[:*digits*]], where the optional *width* specifies the minimum number of characters in the output and the optional *digits* specifies the number of digits to the right of the decimal point for floating-point values. If you do not specify a width for floating-point values, the default is 23.

Example

See FilePos.

Related routines: Append, Assign, IOResult, SetTextBuf, Window, Writeln

Writeln   System

Writes text, variables, and constants to a text file or the screen.

Syntax

PROCEDURE Writeln([VAR *filePointer*: Text;]
    expression: <*simple or component type*>; [...]);

Arguments

filePointer is an optional pointer to a text file that is open for output.

expression is the text or numeric data that Writeln is to put into a file or onto the screen.

Notes

The output formats for Writeln are identical to those used by Write.

Writeln differs from Write in that it supports only text files and in that it writes the carriage-return/linefeed combination at the end of each line.

Example

See Append.

Related routines: Append, Assign, IOResult, SetTextBuf, Window, Write

INDEX TO FUNCTIONS AND PROCEDURES BY UNIT

Crt Unit

AssignCrt   42
ClrEol   50
ClrScr   51
Delay   57
DelLine   59
GotoXY   130
HighVideo   133
InsLine   138
KeyPressed   143
LowVideo   148
NormVideo   159
NoSound   159
ReadKey   182
Sound   239
TextBackground   245
TextColor   246
TextMode   247
WhereX   252
WhereY   253
Window   253

Dos Unit

DiskFree   60
DiskSize   61
DosExitCode   65
DosVersion   66
EnvCount   73
EnvStr   73
Exec   77
FExpand   79
FindFirst   83
FindNext   85
FSearch   92
FSplit   93
GetCBreak   98
GetDate   101
GetEnv   103
GetFAttr   104
GetFTime   108
GetIntVec   114
GetTime   120
GetVerify   121
Intr   140
Keep   142
MsDos   157
PackTime   165
SetCBreak   207
SetDate   210
SetFAttr   211
SetFTime   216
SetIntVec   217
SetTime   227
SetVerify   228
SwapVectors   244
UnpackTime   249

MSGraph Unit

_Arc   37
_Arc_wxy   38
_ClearScreen   48
_DisplayCursor   62
_Ellipse   67
_Ellipse_w   69
_Ellipse_wxy   72
_FloodFill   87
_FloodFill_w   89
_GetActivePage   94
_GetArcInfo   95
_GetBkColor   97
_GetColor   99
_GetCurrentPosition   100
_GetCurrentPosition_wxy   101
_GetFillMask   105
_GetFontInfo   107
_GetGTextExtent   109
_GetGTextVector   109
_GetImage   110
_GetImage_w   112
_GetImage_wxy   113
_GetLineStyle   114
_GetPhysCoord   116
_GetPixel   117
_GetPixel_w   117
_GetTextColor   118
_GetTextCursor   118

_GetTextPosition 119
_GetTextWindow 120
_GetVideoConfig 122
_GetViewCoord 124
_GetViewCoord_w 125
_GetViewCoord_wxy 126
_GetVisualPage 127
_GetWindowCoord 128
_GetWriteMode 129
_GrStatus 130
_ImageSize 134
_ImageSize_w 135
_ImageSize_wxy 136
_LineTo 145
_LineTo_w 147
_MoveTo 155
_MoveTo_w 156
_OutGText 163
_OutMem 164
_OutText 164
_Pie 168
_Pie_wxy 170
_Polygon 171
_Polygon_wxy 173
_PutImage 177
_PutImage_w 178
_Rectangle 184
_Rectangle_w 186
_Rectangle_wxy 187
_RegisterFonts 188
_RemapAllPalette 190
_RemapPalette 192
_ScrollTextWindow 200
_SelectPalette 203
_SetActivePage 205
_SetBkColor 205
_SetClipRgn 208
_SetColor 209
_SetFillMask 212
_SetFont 213
_SetGTextVector 216
_SetLineStyle 218
_SetPixel 219
_SetPixel_w 220
_SetTextColor 222
_SetTextCursor 223
_SetTextPosition 224
_SetTextRows 225

_SetTextWindow 226
_SetVideoMode 229
_SetVideoModeRows 230
_SetViewOrg 231
_SetViewport 232
_SetVisualPage 234
_SetWindow 235
_SetWriteMode 236
_UnRegisterFonts 250
_WrapOn 254

System Unit

Abs 33
Addr 34
Append 35
ArcTan 41
Assign 41
BlockRead 43
BlockWrite 46
ChDir 46
Chr 48
Close 49
Concat 52
Copy 53
Cos 54
CSeg 55
Dec 56
Delete 58
Dispose 64
DSeg 67
Eof 74
Eoln 75
Erase 75
Exit 78
Exp 79
FilePos 80
FileSize 82
FillChar 82
First 86
Flush 90
Frac 90
FreeMem 91
GetDir 102
GetMem 115
Halt 132
Hi 133
Inc 136
Insert 137

Int 139
IOResult 141
Last 143
Length 144
Ln 147
Lo 148
Mark 149
MaxAvail 150
MemAvail 152
Member 153
MkDir 153
Move 154
New 158
Odd 160
Ofs 161
Ord 162
ParamCount 166
ParamStr 167
Pi 168
Pos 174
Pred 176
Ptr 176
Random 179
Randomize 180
Read 181
Readln 183
Release 189

Rename 194
Reset 195
Rewrite 196
RmDir 197
Round 198
RunError 199
Seek 201
SeekEof 201
SeekEoln 202
Seg 202
SetTextBuf 221
Sin 237
SizeOf 238
SPtr 239
Sqr 240
Sqrt 241
SSeg 241
Str 242
Succ 243
Swap 243
Trunc 248
Truncate 248
UpCase 250
Val 251
Write 254
Writeln 255

Kris Jamsa

Kris Jamsa graduated from the United States Air Force Academy with a degree in computer science in 1983. Upon graduation he moved to Las Vegas, Nevada, where he began work as a VAX/VMS system manager for the U.S. Air Force. In 1986 Jamsa received a master's degree in computer science, with an emphasis in operating systems, from the University of Nevada, Las Vegas. He then taught computer science at the National University in San Diego, California, for one year before leaving the Air Force in 1988 to begin writing full-time. He is the author of more than a dozen books on DOS, OS/2, Windows, hard-disk management, and the Pascal and C programming languages. His titles from Microsoft Press include *Microsoft QuickPascal Programming, Graphics Programming with Microsoft C and Microsoft QuickC, Microsoft C: Secrets, Shortcuts, and Solutions,* and numerous quick reference guides. Jamsa resides in Las Vegas with his wife and their two daughters.

The manuscript for this book was prepared and submitted to
Microsoft Press in electronic form. Text files were processed
and formatted using Microsoft Word.

Cover design by Thomas A. Draper
Interior text design by Darcie S. Furlan
Principal typography by Carolyn Magruder
Color separations by Wescan Color Corporation

Text composition by Microsoft Press in Times Roman with
display in Futura Heavy, using the Magna composition system
and the Linotronic 300 laser imagesetter.